# The Long & Winding Trail to Jamestowne, Virginia 1607

# The Long & Winding Trail to Jamestowne, Virginia 1607

Only known portrait of Pocahontas rendered from life.

ONE AFRICAN AMERICAN FAMILY'S DESCENT FROM
JOHN ROLFE & POCAHONTAS THROUGH
EDWARD YATES HAMLIN AND DOLLIE SCOTT OF
DINWIDDIE, VIRGINIA

# Wilhelmena Rhodes Kelly
## and
# Linda Rhodes Jones

**To order additional copies of this book, contact:**
Xlibris LLC
1-888-795-4274
www.Xlibris.com
Orders@Xlibris.com
80208

# Contents

In Loving Memory of Our Mother
**Dorothy Hamlin Rhodes**
1924 – 2010

# Special Thanks

The following family history represents decades of work and commitment. No endeavor of this kind can be accomplished without the critical assistance of family, friends, and keepers of records. This is to acknowledge the willing contributions of our cousins Delia Munford Rose, Ralph Rose, La Verne Mason Earley, Muriel Hughes Burrell, Walter Yates Boyd, and Mark W. Wright.

The earliest search for family information was initiated by our uncle, John W. Hamlin, and his sister Dorothy Hamlin Rhodes of the John W. Hamlin line, who together hired a genealogist back in the 1970s. This provided us with a report that served as an initial foundation for our search.

The enthusiastic cooperation of the Richmond Public Library staff, librarians at the Daughters of the American Revolution headquarters, genealogy staff at the New York Public Library Fifth Avenue branch, and the Dinwiddie Courthouse Archivists is also appreciated.

A special thank you is also owed to family members who sent never-before-seen photos of relatives and members of the many Hamlin-Scott family lines.

Readers who wish to add to the ongoing body of knowledge regarding the Hamlin/Scott family lines are invited to contact Wilhelmena Rhodes Kelly at mena23219@msn.com or Linda Rhodes Jones at lmrhojo@optimum.net with questions, corrections, or new documentation or images.

# Introduction

"EVERYDAY YOU MAY MAKE PROGRESS. EVERY STEP MAY BE FRUITFUL. YET THERE WILL STRETCH OUT BEFORE YOU AN EVER-LENGTHENING, EVER-ASCENDING, EVER-IMPROVING PATH. YOU KNOW YOU WILL NEVER GET TO THE END OF THE JOURNEY. BUT THIS, SO FAR FROM DISCOURAGING, ONLY ADDS TO THE JOY AND GLORY OF THE CLIMB."

Winston Churchill

These words penned by British Prime Minister Churchill in 1922 referenced his ongoing desire to perfect his painting skills, but struck me as applicable to any daunting quest that at first seems insurmountable. When my sister Linda and I began the journey of discovery in our search for Hamlin ancestry, we started with little more than a bit of oral history, the name of our maternal grandfather—John Francis Hamlin (b. 1899), the name of his father—John W. Hamlin(b. 1870), and the fact that the family was rooted in Dinwiddie, Virginia. We could hardly fathom at that time that our search would not only take us back to our Revolutionary War Patriot—Stephen H. Hamlin, but also ultimately lead to the discovery of a paper trail proving our descent from John Rolfe (b. 1585) and Pocahontas (b. 1595). This accomplishment was noteworthy given the more than 400-years distancing us from that time, but made even more remarkable because we are a family of color.

The reasons for writing this book are twofold: to provide a documented history for Hamlin descendants, and to encourage others to begin their own journey of discovery, regardless of how little they presently know about their family history. There are thousands of descendants of John Rolfe and Pocahontas, ancestors just waiting to be discovered under the persistent efforts of the family genealogist. And we, as African Americans, need to be aware of our long presence in this country and willing sacrifices made on its behalf. This provides us with a foundation of knowledge that will not only center us, but also confirm our contributions to the quiltwork of the American fabric.

Electronic resources and data banks such as ancestry.com, familysearch.org (to mention only two), as well as available land and municipal records have made what was once a huge challenge a manageable task we can approach with new confidence. In fact, the biggest challenge at present is to simply begin the journey. It is now up to you the interested reader, to take the first step.

# Chapter 1

## THE BEGINNING

The Edward Yates Hamlin & Dollie Scott Union
1849—Dinwiddie, VA

---

Edward Hamlin (b. 1813) and Dollie Scott (b. 1833) coexisted in a rural household of early 19th century Dinwiddie, Virginia, but lived in two very different worlds.

Edward, known more commonly as 'Ned,' was the son of an affluent, landed family that had resided in Virginia from its early 17th century founding; and Dollie Scott was an enslaved woman of color who was owned by Ned's father, William B. Hamlin, most likely from her birth.

In spite of the 20-year gap in their ages, their racial differences, and Dollie's station at the bottom rung of the social ladder, Ned and Dollie would create a life together that we, from the distance of centuries, cannot fully fathom. Ned never legally took a wife, and Dollie remained in the household—having children both before and after the Civil War—even after the 1863 national Proclamation emancipated her. From the birth of their first known daughter in 1849 to Ned's death in 1878, the two apparently remained a committed couple, with Ned leaving household items and 123 acres of property to her in a will written in 1867.

Precious little is known about Dollie. There is no record of her death, no location of her burial, and no concrete documentation of her origins. We do find a Sallie Scott (mulatto woman born in 1800) sharing the surname, and living in the same household with Dollie through their entire lifetimes. A death record was found for Sallie on the 1884 Dinwiddie death record, but no such paper exists for Dollie who we believe was most likely Sallie's daughter given their comparable ages and on-going presence in the family unit. The 1870 and 1880 Virginia census for Namozine District documents this Hamlin matriarch.

The decades long search continues for the Scott line which will most likely emerge from records of slave sales, slave births, or extant wills perhaps hidden—even today—in antique cupboards and family bibles that have yet to see the light of day. It is hoped that ongoing web postings of new findings will provide a pathway to their past.

Ned, however, has a well-documented family history. It is through his mother—Mary Deane Yates, that we connect to our Pocahontas and John Rolfe 17th century lineage. The history of that descent is detailed in the following pages. Ned's Hamlin line is comprised of a long family line of barristers, local sheriffs, and lawyers, and highlighted by an early presence as representatives in the House of Burgess—Virginia's earliest governing body.

Edward was also trained in the law, and records show he graduated from Hampden-Sydney College in 1833. This training made it possible for him to write a will that protected Dollie and their children after his death.

His mother, Mary Yates, was the third wife of his father William B. Hamlin, and daughter of Elizabeth Murray (b. 1768, VA) and Edward Randolph Yates (b. 1764, VA). It is this line that descends from John Rolfe and Pocahontas, with Yates and Hamlin family facts confirmed by our membership in both the Jamestowne Society and the National Society Daughters of the American Revolution (aka DAR).

A Hamlin/Scott family reunion in 1992 included a visit to the original homestead that Ned, Dollie and their children shared through the 1850s, 1860s, and 1870s (photo above). As of February 2011, this remaining structure, barn (not shown), and overgrown grounds have since been sold and cleared, leaving no remaining trace of their 19th century residence.

# Chapter 2

## LOOKING BACK—LOST HAMLIN RECORDS

Stephen H. Hamlin,
Revolutionary War Patriot 1753

---

The full documentation of the Hamlin family and their presence in colonial Virginia will unfortunately never be achieved. Fires, floods, and particularly the American Civil War destroyed many of the land records and wills that would have provided an unbroken paper trail for this family. Indeed, a lot exists, but still more is unfortunately missing—particularly for our line.

The Hamlin clan once owned thousands of acres in the counties of Mecklenburg, James City, Dinwiddie, Lunenburg, Amelia, Chesterfield, and Prince George Counties, with Dinwiddie officially designated as a 'burned county.' It is primarily through tracing adjacent family histories that we confirmed certain hidden ties.

Starting from known family lines, Edward Yates Hamlin (b. 1813) was the son of Mary Deane Yates of Lunenberg, Virginia and the third wife of William Browne Hamlin of Dinwiddie, Virginia. The Hamlin link to Pocahontas is through the Yates family ancestors, and a generation-by-generation accounting of the Yates connection will be covered in the next chapter.

The Hamlin presence is also one that dates the family back to Jamestowne, Virginia as alchemists, tobacconists, and planters as early as 1634. A small book titled, "House By The Water" written by Griffith A. Hamlin, details the earliest history of the first Hamlins to leave their town of Cornwall in England for relocation to Jamestowne, Virginia. It reveals that Stephen Hamelyn and wife Agnes Turner arrived on the Sunrise on October 22, 1634, and that brother James Hamlin left for Massachusetts five years later.

After laboring and prospering as a Planter for nearly 20 years, Stephen was elected to speak for the people of Charles City County (later Prince George country) in 1655 as a member of the House of Burgess. His son, militia Captain John Hamlin, would follow in his father's footsteps in

1715 when he was elected to the House of Burgesses representing the same county of Prince George.

The Hamlin history contained in the Griffith Hamlin book traces the family's ancestry from their Hamelin roots in Germany in the 900s, to their 1066 Hamelin entry into England with William the Conqueror, the 1570 birth of John Hamlyn, and their departure for America in 1634 and beyond. The chart below, courtesy of www.thehamlins.org/roots/dates.html, details a portion of that history.

## The European Ancestry 900-1638

900s Some Hamelin families moved from Germany to France.
1066 Hamelins entered England with William the Conqueror
1094 Hamelin recorded on roll of Battle Abbey Church
1260 Sir William Hamlyn, Member of Parliament
1311 Robert Hamlyn, Member of Parliament
1570 Birth of John Hamlyn in England

## America

1638 Stephen Hamlyn (?-1665) settled on 250 acres of land on Queen's Creek between Williamsburg and Yorktown.
1642: Obtained additional 400 acres on Queen's Creek.
1650: Obtained 1250 acres south of James River.
1654-1663: Served in the House of Burgesses.
1666 Stephen Hamlyn, Jr. (?-1687) patented 1400 acres south of James River. Married Mary Elam.
**\*1694 Captain John Hamlin (1670-1750) married Elizabeth Taylor. Her brothers owned Flowerdew plantation.**
**\*1723 Captain John Hamlin, Jr. (c1700-1783) sold Maycock plantation. Married Ann Goodrich, 1725. Moved to Namozine Creek near Blackstone, Va.**
**\*1755 Charles Hamlin(1732-??) purchased 674 acres near Nottaway River in Lunenburg County.**
1757: Married Agnes Cocke

The descendants of Ned and Dollie share the Hamlin history of the above chart until we reach the critical juncture (starred and bolded) of Captain John Hamlin (1670-1750). His presence on the Namozine Creek places him in the right location (later known as Dinwiddie), but at issue is the absence of a complete listing of his children with his first and only known wife, Elizabeth Taylor. Our line does not descend from son Captain John Hamlin, Jr. (b. 1732), but through another son born in the

1830s who fathered Revolutionary War Patriot Stephen H. Hamlin (b. 1753). This missing bit of information is the last remaining piece of our Hamlin-Scott family puzzle.

What we do know is that the missing parent for this generation begat son Stephen Henry Hamlin who married Mary Browne. They became parents of William Browne Hamlin (b. 1774) who in turn fathered Edward Yates Hamlin (Ned) through his October 5, 1810 marriage to Mary Deane Yates. They were also the parents of Ned's siblings: Susan Hamlin and William B. Hamlin, Jr.

Over the years, William B. married four times. First to Christian "Kitty" Burwell in 1794; Martha Goode in 1799 and had a daughter Mary Ann Hamlin, who married Samuel Pryor; third wife, Mary Yates who was Ned's mother; and, fourth wife, Anner Patrick Boisseau c. 1825 in Amelia and had a son, James B. Hamlin.

William B. Hamlin, along with his two brothers John F. (b. 1779) and Stephen (b.1776) were the sons of Revolutionary War patriot Stephen Henry Hamlin (b. 1753) of Prince George County. As a farmer, Stephen H. is documented as providing certain critical goods in support of the American Revolution. These included: 1 horse (age 6 years), 3 "beeves" (750 lbs. of beef), 3 sheep, 135 bushels of corn, 600 pounds of fodder and an additional 590 bushels of corn.

The long descent of earliest Hamlin relatives tracing to Ned, his siblings, half-brother and-sisters, and cousins is extensive and is reportedly cast across every state in the union. This text is an effort to determine the fate and movements of the Hamlin/Scott line, much of which had been lost over the last 120+ years since the passing of Ned and Dollie. Following are images of two of Edward Yates Hamlin's first cousins. It is hoped that we might gain some consistent likenesses given the absence of Hamlin and Scott renderings from the early 18th century.

1st Cousin of Ned - Edward Randolph Yates III
(son of Edward Randolph Yates, Jr - brother to Mary Dean Yates
Hamlin, Ned's mom)
b. 25 December 1815-d. 5 January 1904.
Moved to California during Gold Rush and remained there.

Son of John F. Hamlin: Thomas B. Hamlin (b. 1818) was
the nephew of William B. Hamlin and Ned's first cousin.

# Chapter 3

## THE PAPER TRAIL TO JAMESTOWNE, VIRGINIA

### Founded 1607

---

The Hamlin-Scott line can trace its ancestry back to the union of Pocahotas and John Rolfe starting with the April 5, 1614 marriage of the couple. This lineage has been confirmed by the Jamestowne Society, an educational, historical, and patriotic organization dedicated to discovering and recording the names of those early settlers, recording their deeds, and promoting the restoration of historical records and artifacts.

Thousands of Americans share family roots with this world-famous couple, but only a small percentage of the population has committed to uncovering their possible remarkable link with the past.

Although Stephen Hamlin arrived in Jamestowne, Virginia in 1634, and is recognized as one of the earliest settlers of the colony, it is through Edward Yates Hamlin's mother—Mary Dean Yates—that the family has a blood line to Pocahontas.

Wills, land patents, and deeds, as well as death and birth records in family bibles and municipal vaults document this descent. The chart below lists the precise parentage that carried each generation forward. The bottom of the chart shows Ned's father, William B. Hamlin (descendant of Stephen Hamlin of Cornwall, England) married to his third wife, Mary Yates of Lunenberg, Virginia.

However, to more easily follow the Hamlin link with Ned and Dollie, we will begin with Pocahontas at the top of the family chart and work our way down toward the present.

The following account was to a large degree researched and documented by Walter Yates Boyd, Esq. who not only generously shared his Yates and Hamlin family research, but also gave his permission for us to publish his findings for our readers.

Bolded names represent the Hamlin/Scott links.

John Bolling

Mary Kennon wife of John Bolling

Robert Bolling

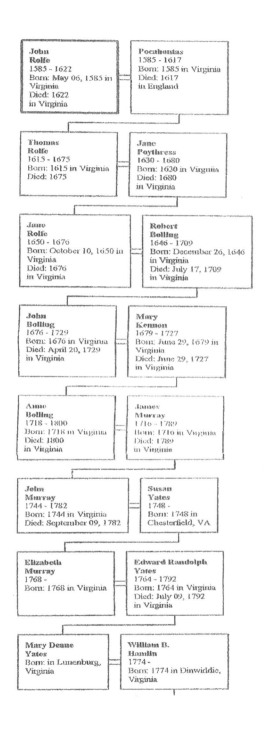

# The Pocahontas Connection

The marriage of Pocahontas and John Rolfe was short lived. During their brief 3-year marriage, they had one child—Thomas Rolfe b. 30 January 1615. As many reader already know, the couple and their son traveled to visit England where Pocahontas died in 1617 shortly before her planned return to Virginia.

Subsequently, Thomas remained there and was raised in England by his uncle Henry Rolfe, a merchant. Upon reaching maturity, he returned to Virginia in 1640 to claim his inheritance, and remained there until his death in 1675. Thomas Rolfe married a Virginian, Jane Poythress (b. 1630) and had one child—Jane Rolfe (b. October 10,1650), the only grandchild of Pocahontas.

At maturity, Jane married Robert Bolling in 1675 and died one year later in 1676, the same year her son John Bolling was born. She and her husband lived at her father's plantation, "Kippax," located just outside Richmond. With her passing, her son John was Pocahontas' only great-grandchild.

Following Jane's death, widower Robert Bolling—a Londoner (b. 1646) who had moved to Virginia fifteen years earlier in 1660—then married Anne Stith. His descendants by first wife Jane (the Hamlin/ Scott line) are known as "Red Bollings" since they are descendants of Pocanhontas. His descendants by Anne Stith are known as "White Bollings" since they have no Indian blood.

At this point, we are three generations removed from Pocahontas, and her great grandchild—John Bolling—is the only living descendant of Pocahontas and John Rolfe. The family tree would soon branch dramatically, however, with John's marriage December 29, 1697 to Mary Kennon of "Conjurer's Neck" in Henrico County. (See generation 4 on the above chart.)

In the ensuing years, John and Mary would have at least six children, and perhaps one or two more who have not been documented. They included: Penelope (1698), John Bolling (b. 1699), Jane Bolling (b. 1703), Elizabeth Bolling (b. 1709), Mary Bolling (b.1711), Martha Bolling (b. 1713), and **Anne Bolling** (b. 1718—d. 1800). From this point on, Pocahontas' descendants increase remarkably as all the children of John Bolling and Mary Kennon Bolling would reach adulthood and have children of their own. Their youngest daughter Anne connects to the Hamlin-Scott line.

Anne Bolling married James Murray and had seven children. The Virginia Bristol Parish register shows the birth of their offspring: James

(1743), **John** (1744), Anne (1746), Margaret (1748), William (1752), Mary (1754), and Thomas (1757) Murray.

Anne and James' son, John Murray (b. 1744) married Susan Yates in 1766 in Prince George County and died at 38 year of age in August 1782 leaving seven minor children: William (1767), **Elizabeth** (1768), Ann (1770), Susanna (1772), James (1774), Margaret (1776), and John, Jr. (1778). His illness seems to have come upon him abruptly because he took the Oath of colonel on July 8, 1782, the same year as his death.

His will specified that his children were to receive two-thirds of his estate to be equally divided, but division could not be made until Elizabeth married or reached the age of 21. This may have led to his daughter marrying the following year to her first cousin, Edward Randolph Yates, perhaps so her father's estate could be more easily settled.

The blood relationships between Elizabeth Murray and cousin Edward Randolph Yates can be traced through Elizabeth's mother, Susan Yates Murray (b. 1748-d.1793).The marriage of cousins was not a rare event in the 1700s. It not only kept accumulated wealth within the family, since the bride often signed off her assets to her future husband at the time of their official engagement; but marriage also united families of like minds, cultures and religions.

The union of Elizabeth Murray (the daughter of Susan Yates Murray) and Edward Randolph Yates (the son of Susan's brother, William Yates, Jr.) also meant the couple shared the same grandparents: Rev. William Yates (b. 1720-1764) and Elizabeth Randolph Yates (b. 1724-1783).

Their grandfather, Reverend William Yates, was the son of the Rev. Bartholomew Yates and wife Sally, and studied the ministry at the College of William & Mary in Williamsburg at about 1738. He traveled to England for his ordination as an Anglican minister in 1745, and in a separate ceremony the following day, was licensed to preach in Virginia.

Between his ordination as a deacon (March 24, 1744/45) and a priest (March 31, 1745), William Yates wed Elizabeth Randolph with a marriage license issued by Edmund Gibson, then Lord Bishop of London. Elizabeth, although born and raised in England, was the daughter of Captain Edward "Ned" Randolph of Virginia, who was the son of William Randolph and Mary Isham considered to be the "Adam and Eve of Virginia" given their numerous progeny. (Their descendants include Thomas Jefferson, John Marshall and Robert E. Lee, who in turn, relate to Hamlin/Scott descendants, as well.)

Directly following their March 27, 1745 wedding, William Yates traveled back to Virginia with new wife Elizabeth Randolph Yates, where they reared a family of seven children: Edward Randolph Yates (b. 1746-1773), **Susanna 'Susan' Yates** (b.1747-1794), Sarah Yates (b.

1748-1757), Elizabeth Randolph 'Betsy' Yates (c.1748-1772), **William Yates, Jr.** (b. 1749-1789), Clara Yates (b. 1750-1832) and Mary Yates (b. 1751-1760).

In 1761, the Reverend William Yates was appointed rector of Abingdon Parish, and later, on February 9, 1761, was unanimously chosen minister of Bruton Parish where he served for approximately five years. Only a month later, he became permanent rector of rector of Bruton Parish, and was appointed the fifth President of William & Mary College on March 10, 1761 where he served for three years (1761-1764).

Nineteen years after his 1764 passing, his grandchildren Elizabeth Murray and Edward Randolph Yates, the son and daughter of his children Susanna and William Yates (bolded above), would marry in 1783. Elizabeth and Edward produced two daughters of record: Elizabeth Yates, and Mary (Deane) Yates.

Mary became the third wife of William B. Hamlin and the mother of Edward Yates Hamlin (b. 1813)—father of our Hamlin/Scott line. Chapter 4 details the biographies of their 12 Hamlin/Scott children.

# Chapter 4

## THE EDWARD YATES HAMLIN / DOLLIE SCOTT DESCENDANTS

### Their Children, Their Lives

---

The search for Ned and Dollie's children was not an easy one. Many were born before men and women of color were documented by name and accurate age. The 1870 Virginia census was the first to list both the free and formerly enslaved on the Federal census records. Given this limitation, and as far as we can determine, Ned & Dollie had 12 children with the following estimated birth dates: **Margaret** b. 1849, **Emma** b. 1850, **Jim** b. 1854, **Mary Elizabeth** (Bettie) b.1857, **Robert** b. 1858, **Horace** b. 1860, **Albert** b. 1862, **Edgar** b. 1864, **Patrick** b. 1866, **Elvira** b. 1869, **John** W. b. 1871, and **Walter** b. 1878. Some of these offspring have been lost to time, and others to circumstances of war, fire and flood.

Jim was apparently never documented again after being listed as a child of Dollie Scott at his birth in 1854 under "Virginia Slave Births." In addition, oral history has it that their son Patrick 'died young' before having children, and that sister Bettie passed away sometime before the 1900 census leaving three young children. Horace also died in circa 1900.

What little may be known about the lives of their ten surviving siblings is detailed below, much of it gleaned from federal census reports. In some cases, photos of their children (or sometimes even grandchildren) were the only images that could be found for a descending line. The following profiles of Ned and Dollie's offspring are listed in order of their birth, and in a number of cases, limited in depth and scope by the lack of oral history and/or family documentation.

# MARGARET SCOTT HAMLIN-c.1849-d.post-1883-Virginia

Margaret Scott Hamblin

The first known child of Ned Hamlin and Dolly Scott—Margaret Scott Hamlin (b. 1849), alternately known as 'Puss' and 'Emma,'—married Wesley Hughes in Dinwiddie, Virginia on December 28, 1867. Over the years, the couple had five children: Sallie, Fannie, Violet, Annie and Edward Yates Hughes. In 1870, Wesley (30) and Margaret (21) are living next door to Margaret's parents, and her siblings: Mary A, Robert, Horace, Albert, Edgar, Patrick and Elvira.

Margaret's son Edward Yates Hughes b. 1883 (pictured next) married Maude Fletcher in 1912 in Richmond, Virginia and produced a family of four children: Hazel, Edward, Elsie and Beverly.

Their daughter, Hazel Hughes (b. 1913 Va.-d. 1996 Washington, DC) married James Mason in 1934 (Washington, DC) and had daughter LaVerne Cecilia Mason b. 1935 in Wash, DC. A close examination of the photo below shows the infant Laverne swathed in a blanket on the lap of her grandfather, Edward Yates Hughes.

Granddaddy hughes
Edward Yates Hughes(b.1883 Dinwiddie-d. 1976 Newport News, VA)

## EMMA HAMLIN—b. 1850-d. 18__

Although no images apparently survive of this second child of Ned and Dollie, records show that Emma had a daughter Novella b. 1868 who in turn had a son George Hamlin b. 1903 (pictured next). He later married Louise Frances Prior April 6, 1924 and over the years the couple had 9 children, eight girls and one boy. Immediately after marrying, George and Frances moved to Pittsburgh, and by 1930 are listed on the Pennsylvania federal census with their children.

As to the final demise for George's mother, Novella: a mortality record for an "Ella Lee," whose age is consistent with Novella's, shows an April 26, 1903 date of death in Richmond and an April 30 burial in Amelia. She was listed as single and employed as a laundress. Further research may prove this to be Emma's daughter, Novella Hamlin.

George Hamlin, Sr. b. 1 March 1, 1903—d. May 1982
Grandson of Emma Hamlin
Son of Emma's Daughter—Novella Hamlin (d. post-1903)

George's daughter Cecelia Hamlin moved to Toronto, and raised daughter Cynthia Hamlin, where they have resided for the past 25 years.

## MARY ELIZABETH "Bettie" HAMLIN—b. 1857-pre. 1900

In the 1880 census, Bettie is in Amelia, VA and is listed as a 'servant' in the household of Armistead Branch and David Royal. She married John T. Lee in Dinwiddie, Virginia on January 2, 1884. Emma was the mother of three children: Cora Lottie, John and Gertrude, and had already passed away by the 1900 Virginia census where husband John is shown as a widow with their son and two daughters. In 1910, John is in Suffolk, Virginia with the two younger children: John (18) and Gertrude (15). That same year, daughter Lottie is in Richmond, working as a cook in the George Font household, along with cousin Sallie E. Hill who was employed as a maid.

Gertrude Lee (2nd from right), the daughter of Mary Elizabeth (Bettie) Hamlin with her cousins in 1980. Mildred, granddaughter of Horace Hamlin (2nd from left), and the four granddaughters of John W. Hamlin (left to right) Wilhelmina, Thelma, Irene and Dorothy.

## ROBERT HAMLIN—b.1858—d. post-1930

Although Robert Hamlin had no children of his own, he played a prominent role in the lives of his sisters and brothers, as well as their offspring. Known as Uncle Bob to his nieces and nephews, Robert at age 42 married Minnie Jones (age 24) on April 4, 1900. Ten years later, they are listed on the 1910 federal census for Dinwiddie, Virginia, with the grandchild of Robert's sister Emma—George Hamlin, age 7. On the 1920 Virginia census, nephew George (16) is still in the household. His relationship with his "Uncle Bob" was so close that when George filled out his marriage certificate, he listed Robert as his father, and later named his only son "Robert" for the uncle who raised him.

Also included in the 1920 census with Robert and Minnie were two daughters of Robert's brother Edgar—nieces Ella (16) and Minnie (12). By 1930, the nieces have grown and gone, and only the couple is listed in the home.

## HORACE HAMLIN—b. 1860-c. d. Jan 29, 1925-Jan 2, 1889

Horace Hamlin (b. 1860 ) was the sixth and middle child of Ned and Dollie. In 1880, he worked in a corn mill and lived next door to married sister Margaret (aka 'Puss'). He married Sallie Pride (b. 1870) on January 2, 1889 in Dinwiddie, VA, and had five children: James Edward Hamlin (b. 1889), Mary Ann Hamlin (1892), Susie Hamlin (1893), Horace Franklin Hamlin (b. 1894) and Marie (b. 1898). When Horace died between 1898 and 1900, his children were all under the age of 10.

On the 1900 census, his widow Sallie Pride Hamlin is with daughters Susie (7) and Ida M (2) (possibly Marie) living with her 84 year old grandmother Clara Bolling listed as a 'doctress.' Sons James (11) and Horace (5) are with Sallie's sister Mollie and her husband Emmett Bland, a house carpenter.

Ten years later in 1910, daughter Mary Ann (age 18) is now with the Bland family, and sister Marie Hamlin (age 12) with uncle George Pride (age 38) and his wife Maggie (age 27). Horace, Jr. (age 15 ) works as a porter in Washington's Union Station and living with his great grandmother Clara Bolling (age 87). In 1917, James (age 27) is on the WWI Draft Records, single, and working as a laborer for Washington Steel in DC.

Daughters Mary Ann, Susie and Marie eventually marry and start families of their own. Horace, Jr. dies in Washington, DC on January 29, 1925 at age 30 and is buried in Church Road, Virginia. The fate of James is unclear, although in 1930 there is a James Hamlin (37) and wife Minnie (36) in Blackwater, Surry, Virginia with their family of five. Perhaps, this is the son of Horace and Sallie.

In 1920, Sallie is in Petersburg with daughter Althea Holmes (b.1907), son Lee Holmes (b. 1911), new husband Isham Brown, children Althea (age 13) and Lee (age 9) and granddaughter Mildred (4 months). By 1930, she is widowed again with granddaughter Mildred (age 14) and grandson Harvey Purdy (9) in her household.

Sallie Pride with sons James Edward Hamlin and Horace Franklin Hamlin

Daughter Marie Hamlin

Daughter Mary Anne

Daughter Susie Hamlin

## ALBERT JAMES HAMLIN—b. 1862-d. January 22, 1924 Richmond, Virginia

In the years 1870 & 1880, Albert Hamlin is living in Virginia with mother Dollie Scott in Namozine District, Dinwiddie, Virginia.

On January 15, 1890, he married Mattie Griffin and the 1900 census shows him in Richmond with his wife of 10 years, and a lodger named Richard Scott is also in the household (age 34). Given the surname, he is very likely a relative.

Albert worked as a blacksmith to earn a living, and by 1910 he is an instructor in a blacksmith shop, and married to his second wife, Melvina. Records show that the couple wed on December 29, 1909 in Powhatan.

In 1920, Albert is again a widow living in Macon township, Powhatan County with 7 year old daughter Helen Maxine Hamlin, and a Sallie A. Hobson (age 65).

Albert Hamlin and Delia Woodley of Jackson County, Virginia were also the parents to Hester Woodley (b. 1887) and Irene Woodley (b. 1885), both born in Amelia.

## EDGAR YATES HAMLIN—b. 1866-d. circa post-1930

Oral history has it that Edgar Yates Hamlin suffered an incident (either a stroke or accident) that permanently affected his leg. Perhaps, this explains why he became a shoemaker by trade, instead of a farmer as did a number of his other siblings.

Documentation shows he married India Anna Brown (b. 1869) in Amelia on March 31, 1897. Their children were Thomas (12), John (10), Ella (7) and Minnie (3), with grandchild Hiram Brown (9) listed on the 1910 census for Amelia, Virginia.

By 1920, an Edgar Hamlen is listed as a widow on the New York City census living on 135ᵗʰ Street in Harlem with his apparent daughter Rosabelle Collins who works as a servant for a private family, and her husband, Edward P. Collins who is a laborer in a tin factory.

In the 1930 Virginia census he's shown in Amelia with son John, d/L Sallie and five grandchildren.

## ELVIRA 'Ella' HAMLIN—b. 1869-d. pre-January 1906

When Ella Hamlin reached the age of 18, she married Thomas Diggs (age 40) on January 2, 1889. Their daughter, Annie Lucy Diggs, was born that same year, and later at age 16 married local farmer William Jefferson (22 years of age) on April 12, 1905 in Dinwiddie, Virginia.

Annie's mother Elvira had expired within a year of Annie's marriage since records show that her father Thomas Diggs remarried on January 3, 1906 to Ann C. Fitzgerald (age 27). Their union produced several half sisters and brothers for Annie.

By 1920, Annie and William Jefferson had six children of their own: Ella, Sallie, Susie, Julia, William and Thomas Jefferson.

Their daughter Julia married three times, and had three children: Abraham, Julia and William Lee during the 1940s.

## JOHN W. HAMLIN b. 1871-d. 1937 Brooklyn, NY

Rev. John W. Hamlin (standing) & Rev. Beverley J. Fletcher (1859—1959)
Photo taken in Brooklyn, NY

John W. Hamlin, the next-to-youngest child of Ned and Dollie, left his Virginia home while still a young man and never returned to his native roots. At 18, he traveled to West Virginia where he married Frances Walker. He then moved further north: first, to Wayne, Pennsylvania; then Red Bank, New Jersey; and finally settled in Brooklyn, New York by 1916.

A detailed accounting of his life and adjacent family lines was published in 2004 which is currently out of print. As a convenience to our interested readers, a copy of that family history is reprinted as the final chapter of this book.

John became a licensed minister in Wayne, Pennsylvania in 1898 and pastored three churches in three different states. He is pictured here with the Reverend Beverley Jordan Fletcher, John Hamlin's friend, spiritual mentor and relative by marriage: Reverend Fletcher's daughter Maude Fletcher, married Edward Yates Hughes—the son of John Hamlin's sister, Margaret Hamlin Hughes.

## WALTER BENNIE HAMLIN
### b. Jan 1878 Dinwiddie-d. circa 1949

Walter Hamlin was the youngest known child of Ned Hamlin and Dollie Scott. At age 24, he married next-door neighbor Hattie Crawley on April 16, 1902 in Dinwiddie, Virginia and worked as a blacksmith as shown on the 1910 and 1920 censuses, as well as on his 1917 World War I draft records. By the outbreak of World War II, Walter is 64 and living in Richmond as a self-employed gardener.

He and Hattie had five children: Walter, Estoria, Irene, Selma and Ruth. In 1910 Walter's nephew John Hill, who works as a carpenter, and wife Sallie are in the household with Walter, Hattie, and their children.

Walter passed away at age 71. His wife Hattie enjoyed great longevity, and reached the age of 96 before passing away in August 1977.

## Outline Descendant Report for Stephen Henry Hamlin Sr.

1 Stephen Henry Hamlin Sr.
.....+ Mary Browne
.......2 William Browne Hamlin Sr b: 1774, d: 19 Jan 1841
.......    ! + Mary Deane Yates
..........3 **Edward Yates Hamlin** b: Abt. 1814 in Dinwiddie County, VA,
              d: Abt. 1878 in Dinwiddie County, VA
.............! + **Dollie Scott** b: 1830
.............4 **Albert James Hamlin** Sr. b: 1865 in Dinwiddie County, VA,
              d: 22 Jan 1924 in Powhatan County, VA
................+ Ella Malvina Howell b: 22 Apr 1881, d: 15 Apr 1918
...................5 Helen Maxine Hamlin b: 20 Jun 1912 in Powhatan
                 County, VA, d: 13 Jul 2001 in Philadelphia, Pa
....................+ Louie Woods
....................5 Albert James Hamlin Jr. d: 1914
.....................  + Delia Woodley d: 28 Dec 1943
....................5 Hester Woodley Davis b: 12 Jun 1887 in Amelia
                 County, Va, d: 28 Feb 1986 in Richmond, Va
....................+ William Albert Munford Jr. b: 08 Jun 1876 in
                 Chesterfield, Virginia, d: 11 Jun 1958 in
                 Richmond, Va
.....................6 Willietta Munford b: 07 Jul 1926 in Richmond, Va, d:
                 27 May 2011 in Richmond, Va
.........................+ Frederick James Robinson Sr. b: 18 May 1921 in
                 Richmond, Va, m: Richmond, Va
...........................7 Frederick James Robinson Jr b: 24 Sep 1964 in
                 Richmond, Va
............................! + Anita D. Holland b: 09 Apr 1962 in Morehead
                 City, NC, m: Richmond, Va
..............................8 Christian Shaw Robinson b: 17 Apr 1990
..........................! + Leroy Jones d: 26 Nov 1948
............................7 Leroy Eric Jones Sr. b: 13 Jul 1949 in
                 Richmond, Va, d: 19 Apr 2005 in
                 Richmond, Va
................................+ Emma Hopkins
..................................8 Leroy Eric Jones Jr.
....................................! + Chiquita m: 15 Apr 2006 in
                 Georgia

..................................................9 Noah Alexander Jones b: 17 Dec
2007
..................................................9 Nicolas Eric Jones b: 17 Dec 2007
..................................................8 Kevin Jones
..................................................8 Cherrate V. Jones b: 10 May 1970
..................................................+ Barbara Harris
..................................................8 LeEisha Erika Harris b: 27 Jan 1985
..................................................8 Barbara S. Harris b: 17 Oct 1989
..................................................7 William St. Elmo Jones Sr. b: 25 Jul 1947
in Richmond, Va
..................................................+ Reiko Yamaguchi
..................................................8 Annette Jones
..................................................+ Joan Jones
..................................................8 William St. Elmo Jones Jr.
..................................................8 Brandi Jones
..................................................7 Brenda Lee Jones b: 24 Apr 1946 in
Richmond, Va
..................................................8 Donald Jones b: 01 Jan 1967
..................................................8 Jennifer Lee b: 29 Jun 1979
..................................................8 Christopher Lee b: 10 Jul 1981
..................................................6 Delia May Irene Munford b: 10 Dec 1930 in
Richmond, Va
..................................................+ James Edward Rose Jr b: 11 Dec 1929 in
Amherst Cty, Va, m: 22 Mar 1952
..................................................7 Ralph Eugene Rose b: 29 Mar 1953 in
Fort Lee, Va.
..................................................+ Alisa A Khayyam b: 28 Apr 1965 in
Michigan
..................................................8 Aaliyyah Theresa Khayyam b: 25 Jun
2004 in Nashville, TN
..................................................+ Arrie Marie Benson b: 30 Aug
1957 in Philadelphia, Pa,
m: 16 Feb 1978 in Yuma,
Az
..................................................8 Amber Mercedes Rose b: 06 Aug
1979 in Yuma, Ariz
..................................................+ Solomon Leon "Shawn" Johnson
..................................................9 Sylas Daniel Johnson b: 06
Dec 2005 in Fresno, CA
..................................................+ Gabriel Delsid

.............................................................9 Noah Gabriel Delsid b: 08
May 2002
.............................................................+ Karen Yvonne Jones b: 17
Sep 1957 in
Baltimore, MD, m:
18 Jan 1994
in Baltimore, MD
...............................................7 Albert Keith Rose b: 04 Oct 1954 in
Lynchburg, VA
...............................................+ Gale Taylor
...............................................8 Sade Rose b: 01 Sep 1988 in
Richmond, Va
...............................................+ Karen Griffin
...............................................8 Keyana Griffin b: 31 May 1983 in
Richmond, Va
...............................................7 Kenneth Nathaniel Rose b: 10 Sep 1957 in
Lynchburg, VA
...............................................7 Charles Edward Rose b: 12 Dec 1958 in
Lynchburg, VA
...............................................+ Vernessa Boines b: 30 Apr 1960 in
Brooklyn, NY, m: 28 Dec 1985 in
Queens, NY
...............................................8 Patrick William Rose b: 08 Jul 1986
...............................................8 Nicole Mia Rose b: 02 May 1990
...............................................8 Aaron James Rose b: 20 Aug 1992
...............................................+ Lashawn Durah Forehand b: 31
Jul 1970
...............................................8 Courtney Elanis Rose b: 18 Sep
1999 in Richmond, Va
...........................5 Irene Woodley b: 02 Mar 1895 in Amelia County, Va,
d: Jun 1985 in Richmond, Va
...............................+ Felix Morgan
...............................6 Estelle "Big Sister" Morgan b: 17 Jun 1916 in
Amelia County, Va
...............................+ Henry Clay Hayes
...............................7 Queen Hester Stewart b: 22 Oct 1942
...............................7 Henry J. "Juney" Hayes b: 11 Feb 1940 in
Amelia County, Va
...............................+ Dorothy Mae W. Hayes b: 11 Feb 1940, m:
08 Apr 1960
...............................8 Carolyn Virginia Hayes b: 29 Sep
1964

..............................6 Adelle Morgan

.................................! + William Banks d: 15 Mar 2001 in Richmond, Va

.........................................7 Michael Banks

..............................6 Willie Morgan

..............................6 Phillip Morgan Sr b: 11 Jan 1921 in Amelia
County, Va, d: 20 Sep 1996 in Richmond, Va

..............................+ Daisy Haile

.....................................7 Phillip Morgan Jr b: 01 Jul 1950 in
Washington, DC

..............................6 Benjamin Morgan

..............................6 Robert Morgan

..............................+ Mattie Hamlin

..............4 **Walter Bennie Hamlin** b Jan 1878 m. 16 Apr 1902 d.
1949

.................+ Hattie F. Crawley b. 1881 d. August 1977

.......................5 Walter Stuart Hamlin Sr.

...........................+ Irene Lipscomb

..............................6 Juanita Bernice Hamlin

.....................................+ George P. Armistead III


.........................................7 Charlene Denise Armistead

................................................8 Brittany Christen Mickens

................................................8 Bryten Cymone Mickens.

.....................................7 Pamela Yvette Armistead

..............................6 Walter Stuart Hamlin Jr.

...................................+ Barbara Hamlin

...................................7 LaWonne Hamlin

...................................7 Kellie Rene Hamlin

............................6 Joyce Hamlin Canada

.........................5 Estoria Hamlin

.............................6 Robinette Jones Smith

.........................5 Irene Hamlin b: 30 Jul 1904

.........................+ Robert Lincoln Coots

..........................6 Sylvia Coots b: 25 May 1933

.................................+ Curtis Roosevelt Robinson b: 19 Nov 1932, m: 21
Apr 1957, d: Richmond, Va

.......................................7 Cynthia Robinson b: 01 Feb 1958 in
Richmond, Va.

.............................................+ James A. Temple Jr. m: 14 Jun 1980

....................................................8 Melody Lauren Temple b: 02 May
1985

....................................................8 Micah James Temple b: 07 Jan 1988

...............................................7 Donna R. Mack-Tatum b: 20 Aug 1960
...............................................+ Raymond Tatum m: 14 Apr 1990
.....................................................8 Michelle Mack b: 28 Jun 1985
........................5 Selma Hamlin
..........................5 Ruth Elizabeth Hamlin b: 28 Aug 1913, d: 01 Feb 2000 in
         Richmond, Va
..............................+ Ulysses Lee Sr. b: 03 Oct 1910, d: 30 Nov 1991
...................................6 Barbara Ann Lee b: 09 Jul 1932, d: 25 May 1970
.............................................7 Gene Lee b: 20 Jan 1953
.....................................6 Ulysses Lee Jr. b: 29 May 1934
.......................................+ Ohyeon Kim Lee
...........................................7 Anthony Lee b: 31 Oct 1970
...........4 **Betty Hamlin** b. 1857 d. pre-1900
..............+ John T. Lee 2 Jan
.....................5 Gertrude Hamlin Lee
.....................5 Lottie Hamlin
.....................5 John Hamlin.
.........4 **Margaret Hamlin** b: 1856 c. post-1883
.............+ Wesley Hughes
...................5 Sallie Ann Hughes b: 16 Jul 1888
.....................+ John W. Hill b: 18 Jan 1884
.............................6 Fannie Hill b: 25 May 1931 in Dinwiddie County, VA
.............................+ Edward H. Branch m: 18 Nov 1954
.....................................7 Edwina Branch Howard b: 14 Jul 1957
.....................................7 Pamela R. Branch b: 16 Feb 1959
.............................6 Anna Hill b: 08 Aug 1919
.............................+ Leslie Robert Peterson
.....................................7 Katherine L. Peterson b: 01 Dec 1948 in
         Montclair, NJ
...........................................8 Jeffery K. Peterson b: 20 Aug 1967
.........................6 Olga Hill McKenzie b: 11 Apr 1921
...................5 Fannie Hughes
...................5 Violet Hughes
.....................+ Levi Taylor
...........................6 Leonard Taylor

...................5 Annie Hughes
...........................6 Eugene Hughes
.............................+ Blanche Pearl Brown
.....................................7 Florence E. Hughes
...............................................8 Shirley A. Davis Phillips

...........................................7 Ethel Blanche Hughes b: 22 Feb 1919 in
Richmond, Va, d: 23 Apr 1977 in
Richmond, Va

........................................ + Earl David Johnson b: Wayno, PA, d: 11 Aug
1966 in Sourh Carolina

....................................8 Earl Ronald Johnson b: 10 May 1948

....................................+ Lorraine Edelen

.............................................9 Shaletta Sharrell Johnson
b: 04 Feb 1986

.............................................9 LaRonda Chinelle
Johnson b: 28 Sep 1989

...................8 Rosalind Marie Johnson b: 30 Jun
1949

...................................9 Corey E. Johnson b: 12
May 1969

...........................7 Eugenia L. Hughes Davis

...........................7 Muriel Eulalia Hughes b: 14 Aug 1930

..................................+ Archie Bernest Burrell

.............................................8 Yolanda Yvette Burrell b: 30 Sep
1954

..............................................+ Harold Nathaniel Taylor

.............................................9 Erica Nicole Taylor

.............................................9 Ashley Marie Taylor

...........................7 Hortense L. Hughes b: 10 Aug 1922 in
Richmond, Va

..................................+ Donnie Barnes b: 15 Feb 1919 in North
Carolina, m: 03 Apr 1969 in Washington,
DC, d: 16 Feb 1975 in Richmond, Va

...........................7 Lloyd Vincent Hughes Sr. d: 17 Sep 2006 in
Richmond, Va

..................................+ Alma s. Hughes

.............................................8 Lloyd V. Hughes Jr.

.............................................8 Nichelle Hughes

...........................7 Leonard N. Hughes Sr.

.............................................8 Leornard N. Hughes Jr.

.............................................8 Earl A. Hughes

.............................................8 Karen L. Hughes

.............................................8 Anthony E. Hughes

...........................7 Donald L. Hughes Sr. b: 12 Oct 1932 in
Richmond, Va

..............................+ Avis C. Hughes m: 17 May 1975

..............................+ Mary W. Hughes b: Richmond, Va, m: 26
May 1956 in Richmond, Va

....................................8 LeMoyne C. Hughes b: 07 Oct 1956

....................................8 Donald L. Hughes Jr. b: 31 Jan 1962

....................................8 Gerena M. Hughes b: 02 May 1958,
d: 01 May 1959

.........................7 Fred L. "Dempsey" Hughes

................................8 Sabrina Squire Williams

................................8 Michael E. Hughes

................................8 Velma E. Hughes

................................8 Cynthia L. Hughes

.........................7 Mary Edith Hughes

...............5 Edward Yates Hughes b: 25 Aug 1883 in Dinwiddie, VA, d:
25 Sep 1976 in Amelia, VA

....................+ Maude Fletcher b: 25 Sep 1889 in Dinwiddie, VA, m:
Abt. 1912 in Richmond, Va, d: 16 Jan 1963 in
Washington, DC

........................6 Hazel Hughes b: 15 Apr 1913

........................+ James Mason

..............................7 LaVerne Mason b: 30 Jan 1935 in Washington,
DC

..................................+ Charles Edward Earley Jr. b: 18 Oct 1933 in
Washington, DC, m: 01 Apr 1953 in
Washington, DC

....................................8 Linda Earley b: 06 Nov 1953 in
Washington, DC

....................................+ Mark John Chastang Sr. b: 08
Aug 1952 in Mobile, AL,
m: 30 Aug 1980
in Washington, DC

............................................9 Rebecca Earley
Chastang b: 07
Oct 1985 in
Atlanta, GA

............................................9 Mark John Chastang
Jr. b: 16 May 1983
in Atlanta, GA

....................................8 Dianne Elizabeth Earley b: 22 Jul
1952

...............................................8 Charles Frances Earley b: 05 Dec
1965
...............................................8 David Edward Earley b: 07 Jun
1967
........................................7 Robert Edward Mason b: 05 Apr 1947
........................................+ Judy Murray
...............................................8 John Marshall Mason b: 06 Nov 1972
...............................................8 Jill LaVerne Mason
........................6 Edward Francell Hughes b: 25 Dec 1914
........................6 Elsie Fletcher Hughes b: 14 Aug 1916 in Amelia
County, Va, d: 16 Dec 2002 in Amelia County, Va
............................+ Joseph Barnes
............................7 Joseph Barnes Jr
............................7 Judith Leona Barnes
...............................+ Alexander Datcher Wright
...................................8 Mark Alexander Wright
.......................................+ Leah Nicole Williams m: Mannboro, VA
...............................................9 Noah Alexander Wright
...............................................9 Jacob Daniel Wright b: 16 May 2008
...................................8 Kimberley Wright b: 1964
.......................................+ Frederick Douglass Jones III m: 1991
............................................... 9 Frederick Douglass Jones IV
...............................................9 Matthew Alexander Jones
........................... 6 Beverly J. Hughes b: 19 Jan 1918.
.................................7 Lottie Wallace Hughes
...............................8 Charlotte Hughes
.......................................+ Moses David
............................................... 9 Ida Hughes
.......................................................10 Christopher Donald
...................................9 Catherine David
.......................................+ Anthony Wash
.......................................10 Alexandria Wash
.......................................10 Anthony Wash
...................................9 Raymond David
.......................................10 Fatima David
.......................................10 Mark David
.......................................10 Raena Richardson
..............4 **Horace Hamlin** b. 1860 m. 2 Jan 1889
.................." " + Sally Pride b. 1870
......................5 Mary Ann Hamlin b. 1891
..........................+ William Norman Hamlin
............................6 Doris Hamlin

.....................5 Marie Hamlin b. 1898

..............4 **Edgar Hamlin** b: 1864 m. 31 Mar 1897 Amelia d.
        post-1924

................+India Anna Brown b. 1869

...................5 Minnie Hamlin b: 13 Mar 1907

...................+ M. Coleman

...................5 John Francis Hamlin b: 25 Nov 1898

.....................+ Sally Brown b: 17 Mar 1900

............... 6 Evelyn Hamlin

...........................+ Jessie Hawkes Sr.

...................................7 Carolyn Williams

...................................7 Mary Sue Tucker

...................................7 Viola Person

...................................7 Jessie Hawkes Jr.

...................................7 Kenneth Hawkes

...................................7 Donald Hawkes

...................................7 Vincent Hawkes

...................................7 Brian Hawkes.

............................6 Effie Hamlin Bates

...............................+ Alfred Bates

...................................7 Wallace Bates

...................................7 Eugene Bates

...................................7 Mark Bates

...................................7 Velvet Smith

........................... 6 Thomas Albert Hamlin Sr

...........................+ Hazel Hamlin

................................... 7 Thomas Albert Hamlin Jr.

...................................7 Gwendolyne Henry

...................................7 Lisha Haynes

.........................6 John Walter Hamlin

...........................+ Alice Hamlin

...................................7 Kathleen McKenzie

...................................7 Ella Graham

...................................7 Alice Hamlin

.........................6 James Edward Hamlin Sr

...........................+ Dorothy Hamlin

...................................7 Sandra Hill

...................................7 James Edward Hamlin Jr.

...................................7 Shelia Bowers

...................................7 Kelly Hamlin

...................................7 Joan Hamlin

...................................7 Tony Hamlin

......................................7 Brenda Hamlin
......................................7 Danny Hamlin
......................................7 Valerie Tyler
...........................6 Fannie Hamlin
...............................+ Milton Smith
......................................7 Nancy Lewis
......................................7 Phillis Robertson
......................................7 Mildred Baltimore
...........................6 Annie Hamlin
...............................+ John H. Hembrick
......................................7 Nancy Mayo
......................................7 Mary Briggs
......................................7 Mildred Banks
......................................7 Leslie Hembrick
......................................7 Louis Hembrick Sr.
......................................7 George Hembrick
......................................7 John Hembrick
......................................7 William Russell Hembrick
...........................6 Catherine Hamlin b: 09 Apr 1936 in Mannboro, VA
.......................... + Charles Earl Burns b: 30 Oct 1933, m: 05 Jun 1954
......................................7 Earl Charles Burns b: 03 Oct 1954
......................................7 Michelle Lisa Burns b: 03 Oct 1963
...............................................+ Arnoldo Smith b: 06 Jan 1966, m: 24 Feb
                1990
................................................8 David Daniel Smith b: 11 Apr 1991
......................................7 Janet Denise Burns b: 21 Dec 1965.
...............................................+ Nasser Staples b: 08 Feb 1966, m: 18 May
                1990
......................................7 Chermeine Catherine Burns b: 18 Jul 1967 in
                Bridgeport, CT
...............................................+ Carlos Javier Rivera b: 23 Aug 1966, m: 24 May
                1986
................................................8 Carlos Javier Rivera Jr. b: 11 Oct 1986
................................................8 Ave Renee Rivera b: 16 Feb 1990
...........................6 Mamie Hamlin b: 14 Jan 1945 in Mannboro, VA
...............................+ Allen D. Booker m: 27 Sep 1961
......................................7 Angela Booker b: 16 Mar 1962
...............................................+ Larry Thompson Sr.
................................................8 Larry Thompson Jr.
................................................8 Jason Thompson
......................................7 Sally D. Booker Higgs b: 25 Jul 1972
................................................8 Chaunnette Higgs

...............................................8 Nicholas Higgs
.................................7 Anthony D. Booker b: 23 Apr 1975
.................................7 Elizabeth C. Booker b: 28 Jun 1969
.................................7 Ellen R. Booker
...............................................8 Garrett Booker
...............................................8 John S. Miller IV
.................................7 Cynthia J. Booker
..............5 Thomas Hamlin
..............5 Ella Louise Hamlin b: 13 Mar 1903, d: 16 Sep 1974
...................+ Cecil Burke Clarke m: 30 Dec 1923 in Springfield Bapt
        Church, Dinwiddie, VA.
...................6 Delores Maxine Clarke b: 05 Jan 1935
...........................+ Oneil Howard Wilson Sr. b: 27 Nov 1931, m: 16 Aug
        1952
.................................7 Pansy Oneil Wilson
.................................+ Harold Lee Lewis
...............................................8 Jessica Alexandra Barlow b: 11 Oct 1972
...............................................8 Robert Cornell Barlow
...............................................8 Lorenzo Darnell Barlow
.................................7 Treska Yasmine Wilson b: 02 Nov 1952
................................. + John Edward Smith
...............................................8 Jasmine Oneil Smith b: 11 Sep 1971
...............................................8 John Everette Smith b: 26 Apr 1973
...............................................8 Kendall Wilson Smith b: 11 Oct 1974
.................................7 Joy Wilson Charles b: 01 Apr 1956
.................................+ Roosevelt Leo Charles b: 26 Oct 1954
...............................................8 Misha Jermaine Charles b: 12 Aug 1979
...............................................8 Jeffrey Arhmad Charles b: 22 Sep 1980
...............................................8 Thomas Sinclair Charles b: 12 Jan 1984
.................................7 Oneil Howard Wilson Jr. b: 20 Sep 1958
.................................7 Miguel Wilson b: 20 Feb 1960
.................................7 Jerri Wilson b: 10 Jun 1965
...............................................8 Blake Anthony Wilson b: 09 Mar 1985
...................6 Jerome Curtis Clarke
...................6 Cecil Christine Clarke b: 23 Jun 1931, d: 10 Jun
        1967
...................6 Otis Marshall Clarke
...........4 **Robert Hamlin** b. 1850—d. post-1930
..............+ Minnie A. Hamlin
...........4 **Emma Hamlin**
...................5 Novella Hamlin

..........................6 George Hamlin

.............................+ Frances Pryor

.................................7 Rosa Hamlin McGriff

.................................7 Josephine Hamlin Spencer

.................................7 Jacqueline Hamlin Burnham

.................................7 Ella Hamlin Green

.................................7 Cecelia Hamlin (Toronto, Canada)

.................................Cynthia Hamlin

.................................7 Minnie Ruth Hamlin Glaze

.................................7 Peggy Elston

.................................7 Robert Emette Hamlin b: 04 Oct 1925 in
        Pittsburgh, PA, d: 26 Aug 1991 in Wilkinsburg,
        PA

.................................+ Helen Rogers m: 10 Mar 1950

.......................................8 Ronald Hamlin

.......................................8 Joanne Hamlin

.......................................+ James Smith

.......................................8 R. Elton Hamlin

.......................................8 Bonnie Hamlin

.................................7 Doris Priscilla Hamlin b: 13 Nov 1927.

.................................+ Charles Edward Hite b: 22 Nov 1922 in
        Brunswick County, VA, m: 07 Aug 1954 in
        Blackstone, VA, d: 07 May 1985 in Petersburg,
        VA

.......................................8 Randolph H. Hite b: 01 Sep 1948

.......................................8 Charles F. Hite b: 29 Jun 1958

.............4 **Elvira Hamlin** b: 1869 m. 02 Jan 1889

................+ Thomas Diggs : 1863 in Dinwiddie County, VA

.............4 **John William Hamlin** b: 03 Jun 1871 in Dinwiddie County,
        VA, d: 13 Aug 1937 in Brooklyn, NY

................+ Frances Walker b: 01 Apr 1873

....................5 James Hamlin Hazel Hamlin b: 1906 + Paul Jones

.................... 5

....................5 Susan G. Hamlin b: 01 Apr 1895

....................5

....................5

....................5

.............................6 John William (Dukie) Hamlin b: 04 Apr 1921 in
        Brooklyn, NY, d: 05 Jun 1997

.............................+ Frances E. Hamlin b: 17 Nov 1919, m: 18 Jun
        1943, d: 18 Apr 2008 in John Francis Hamlin b:
        24 Jul 1899, d: 25 Jan 1966 + Wilhelmina

Johnson b: 30 Jul 1903 Brooklyn, NY
.................7 John William Hamlin III b: 23 Apr 1945 in
Brooklyn, NY
.................7 Pamela Inez Hamlin b: 11 Jun 1950 in Brooklyn,
NY
.....................+ Raymond N. Cook m: 27 Aug 1973
...........................8 Allison Monique Cook b: 07 Dec 1978
.................7 Patricia Geneva Hamlin b: 17 Feb 1959 in
Brooklyn, NY
.................7 Leonard L. Hamlin Sr. b: 11 Jul 1960 in Brooklyn,
NY
.....................+ Machell A. Hamlin m: 16 Jun 1984
...........................8 Leonard L. Hamlin Jr. b: 14 Sep 1988
...........6 Dorothy Hamlin b: 19 Dec 1923 in Brooklyn, NY
...............+ George Rhodes m: 09 Oct 1943
.................7 Linda M. Rhodes b: 19 Jul 1944 in Brooklyn, NY
.....................+ Ronald E. Jones m: 06 Jul 1974
...........................8 Melanie Jones b: 17 Aug 1976
.................7 Wilhelmena Rhodes Kelly b: 11 Dec 1946
...........6 Irene Hamlin b: 07 Jul 1925 in Brooklyn, NY
...............+ Frank Jackson Jr. b: 12 Oct 1925, m: 08 Apr 1947
.................7 Rose Elizabeth Jackson b: 13 Aug 1947
.................7 Lance Douglas Jackson b: 28 Jan 1949
.................7 Cheryl Ann Jackson b: 08 Apr 1955
...........................8 Neil Earl Jackson b: 26 Aug 1969
...........6 Thelma Hamlin b: 25 Sep 1927 in Brooklyn, NY
...............+ Austin Francis m: 30 Sep 1962
...............+ Vernon Lawless
.................7 LaVerne Lawless b: 22 May 1950 in Brooklyn, NY
.....................+ Samuel Davids m: 01 Apr 1977
...........................8 Jason Davids b: 08 Mar 1979
...........................8 Michael Davids b: 15 May 1987
...........6 Catherine Hamlin b: 11 Jan 1923 in Brooklyn, NY
...............+ Mitchell H. Bryant m: 23 Oct 1948
.................7 Karen Bryant b: 12 Jan 1958
...........................8 Corey Bryant
.................7 Michael Bryant b: 19 Jan 1952
...........6 Wilhelmina Hamlin b: 31 Mar 1930 in Brooklyn, NY
...............+ George C. Abraham b: 02 Jun 1928, m: 12 Apr 1960
.................7 Adrienne Abraham b: 26 Sep 1960 in Brooklyn, NY
.....................+ Joseph Bonilla m: 11 Jan 1986
...........................8 Joseph Manuel Bonilla b: 28 May 1986

..............................7 Geoffrey C. Abraham b: 18 Jul 1963 in Brooklyn, NY
.............................+ James Washington m: 04 Feb 1949
..............................7 John Robert Washington b: 06 Jul 1951, d: 1989
..............................7 Denise Elizabeth Washington b: 22 Jul 1949
..............................+ John Fred Lee
....................................8 Stacey L. Lee
....................................8 Tracey L. E. Lee
...........................................+ Dwayne Deslandes
..................................................9 Imani Deslandes
..................................................9 Ethan Deslandes
....................................8 Crystal Lee
...........................................9 Elijah D.P. Lee
...........................................9 Aaliyah W. Lee
...........................................9 Demetrious X.M. Lee
................5 Gertrude B. Hamlin b: 26 May 1903.
......................+ Russell F. Greene b: 24 Mar 1905
...........................6 Gertrude B. Greene b: 09 Mar 1927 in Brooklyn, NY
.............................+ William R. Washington Sr. m: 26 Jul 1946
..................................7 William R. Washington Jr. b: 19 Sep 1947
..................................7 Nevin R. Washington b: 07 Dec 1952
..................................7 Pandora B. Washington b: 29 Nov 1955
................5 William Arnold Hamlin b: 11 Aug 1909, d: 24 Apr 1975
....................+ Hattie Elizabeth Hamlin b: 03 Sep 1908, d: 1969
..........................6 Joan Elizabeth Hamlin b: 10 Mar 1927, d: 1983
...........................+ Stanley Harney
...........................7 Melissa Harney
..........................6 Carrol Francis Hamlin b: 13 Oct 1930 in Brooklyn,
            NY, d: 02 Nov 2006
............................+ Elizabeth Knowles m: 27 Sep 1967
..........................6 Paul T. Hamlin
...........................7 Paula Hamlin
..................................+ David A. Parker
.........................................8 Monique S. Parker
.........................................8 Jasmine D. Parker
.........................................8 Chantae A. Parker.
.........................................8 Zachary M. Parker
.........................................8 Marques V. Parker
...........................7 Paul Harris
..........................6 Gregory Hamlin
...........................+ Donna Richardson.
..................................7 William Anthony Hamlin
..................................7 Ashley Hamlin

...........................6 William James Hamlin
...........................+ Betty Babb
...............................7 Gloria Hamlin
...................................8 Shelley Hamlin
...................................8 Danny Hamlin
...................................8 Shawn Hamlin
...............................7 Billy Hamlin Jr
...............................7 Ronald Hamlin
...............................7 Robert Hamlin
...............................7 Kenneth Hamlin
...............................7 Mark Hamlin
...............................7 David Hamlin
...............................7 William Hamlin
.......................6 Pauline Hamlin
...........................+ <Unk> Murphy
...........................+ Elizabeth F. Jackson b: 1917, d: 1993
...............5 Irene E. Hamlin b: 21 Feb 1902, d: 11 Dec 1998
.......................6 Bonnie Hamlin
.........................+ Ron Bazil
...............................7 Tami Bazil
...............................7 Lance Bazil
..........4 **Patrick H. Hamlin** b: 1867
..........4 **Jim Hamlin** b: 05 Mar 1854
......3 William Browne Hamlin Jr
......3 Susan Hamlin
.........+ Anner Boisseau
......3 James Boisseau Hamlin
.........+ Christian Burwelli
.........+ Martha Goode
......3 Mary Anne Hamlin
....2 Stephen Henry Hamlin Jr b: 1778
....2 John Hamlin Esq b: 1779, d: 1824
.......+ Hannah Browne
........3 John F. Hamlin b: 1800
........3 Stephen H. Hamlin b: 1810
........3 Thomas B. Hamlin b: 1818
........3 George W. Hamlin b: 1811

Prepared By: Ralph E Rose
Address: Little Rock, AR
Email: arose4u@msn.com
United States

# *Chapter 5*

## BIBLIOGRAPHY

---

*Adventurers of Purse and Person* (4 Volume Set) 4th Edition 1607-1624/25

*Colonial Wills of Henrico County, Virginia Part One 1654-1737*
Abstracted & Compiled by Benjamin B. Weisiger III

*Early Virginia Immigrants 1623-1666* by George Cabell Greep

*Early Virginia Families Along the James River* by Louise P.H. Foley

*Forgotten Patriots African American and American Indian Patriots of the Revolutionary War* A Guide to Service, Sources and Studies
Eric G. Grundset, Editor
Published by National Society Daughters of the American Revolution

*History of the Colony and Ancient Dominion of Virginia*
by Charles Campbell publ. 1860

*House by the Water* Twelve Generations in Virginia by Griffith A. Hamlin

*Pocahontas alias Matoaka and Her Descendants with Biographical Sketches*
publ. 1887
by Wyndham Robertson

*Quaker Records of Henrico Monthly Meeting* by F. Edward Wright

*Roots for Kids* A Genealogy Guide for Young People by Susan Provost
Beller

*The Old Free State* by Landon Covington Bell

*Virginia Immigrants and Adventurers 1607-1635*—Martha W. McCartney

*The Virginia Magazine of History and Biography,* Volume I published by
Virginia Historical Society, June 1894

*Unrecorded Deeds & Other Documents Amelia County, Virginia 1750-1902*
Abstracted and Compiled by Gibson Jefferson McConnaughey

*Yates* The 300-Year Story of an American Family From England to
Virginia and Beyond.
by Walter Yates Boyd, Jr. (manuscript)

# Chapter 6

## THE SEARCH FOR YOUR ANCESTORS IN
## JAMESTOWNE, VIRGINIA

### A Primer

*"A journey of a thousand miles begins with but a single step."*

Ancient Chinese proverb.

So you say you are interested in locating your Civil War ancestor, or Revolutionary War Patriot, or even a family member who helped settle colonial America. All American families with long roots in the States will find that regardless of where they are living today, all genealogical ties trace back to the original 13 colonies. Virginia was the nation's first colony, founded in 1607, and the Jamestowne Society—a heritage organization whose members link back to those times—has information to help you get there.

But the question is, "Where to begin?"

The answer is simple and invariably the same: Always start with yourself and work back into the past. If you skip even a single generation, you can easily head down the wrong road.

Many begin the search, and then abandon it because the task seems to be beyond their reach. Successful genealogists find that if you focus on just one generation at a time, and one family line at a time, you can make remarkable progress with surprisingly little effort.

Internet availability of vital records—dates and places of births, marriages and deaths—has made it convenient to search for information at home or at your local library. However, staying organized and storing your findings in a single location will help you keep track of your successes. Begin by purchasing a 3-ring binder and stock it with top loading transparent plastic sleeves.  As you locate your family information, store copies of these documents in your binder, and then complete this new information on your family sheets. (A form available for your REFERENCE follows.)

Fill in your name, date and location of your birth, the names of your mother and father, and the names of their parents. Copy your birth certificate (which should show your parents' names), your marriage certificate (if applicable), and the birth and death certificates of both parents. This document should show the names of the decedent's mother and father. This will automatically take you back a generation based upon this confirmed documentation.

At this point, decide whether you want to pursue your maternal or paternal line, and begin your computer search at familysearch.org (a free web site maintained by the Church of Later Day Saints), or at the closest library that subscribes to ancestry.com.

You are now off to a good start. Your mother's or father's certificates will show the names of your grandparents and by typing in their information you can soon locate them on federal census reports as children in the homes of their parents. With luck, the grandparents may be in the household, as well. As you know, the census is taken every ten years, and access to the records from 1790 to 1940 are open to anyone who wishes to view them. There is a 72-year privacy gap in census availability, so in April 2012, the 1940 census information was opened to anyone searching for answers.

When viewing the census reports be sure to note the variety of spellings, the variations in ages from census-to-census, and documented inconsistencies in your oral history. Continue your search with an open mind.

Also, be sure to note the birth dates and locations of the oldest relatives in the household. No colonial families established their beginning in Chicago, Los Angeles, or Detroit. In genealogy, all roads lead to the first American colonies, with the large majority of black families rooted in the South.

This Southern heritage is what will take you to your earliest ancestors and possible Virginia roots. The Old Dominion's earliest settlement at one time included what is today North Carolina, South Carolina, Alabama, Maryland, and even parts of Pennsylvania.

Become familiar with the many common surnames of the oldest southern families like Hamlin, Bolling, Bush, Stainback, Isham, Murray, and Yates. They all were rooted in Virginia before they moved north, south, and west. The most helpful text in this regard is *Adventurers of Purse and Person* 4th Edition 1607-1624/25. It details the genealogy of the south's earliest families. This 4 volume set can be found in most large libraries.

Keep searching until you feel there is nothing more to be found, and then join a Genealogical Society or heritage organization. They will be happy to take you further. African American families have long and deep roots that are among the oldest in the country. Search the European neighbors next door, and don't dismiss the many listings of Free People of Color. Not all black families were enslaved. The book *Free AfricanAmericans of North Carolina, Virginia and South Carolina* by Paul Heinegg is an excellent resource and available on line at freeafricanamericans.com.

For further information on the search for your ancestry, please feel free to contact Wilhelmena Rhodes Kelly at mena23219@msn.com or Linda Rhodes Jones lmrhojo@optimum.net. We will be happy to assist you, or direct you to someone who can.

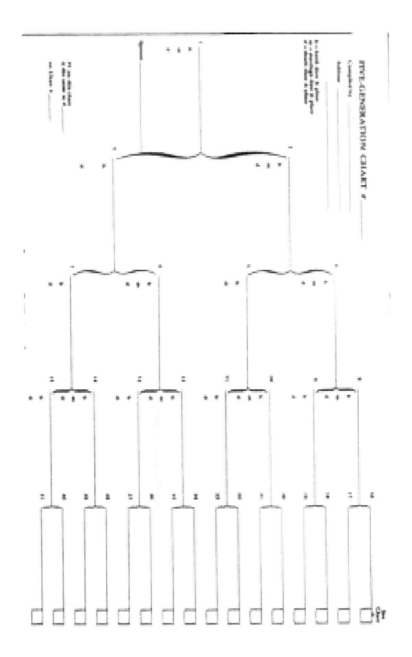

# Chapter 7

## JOHN W. HAMLIN OF DINWIDDIE
## COUNTY, VIRGINIA

His Ancestors and Descendants
1753-2004

---

### (Reprint)

In 2004, a small booklet was published detailing family descendants of Edward Yates Hamlin and Dollie Scott providing documentation dating back as far as Stephen H. Hamlin (b. 1753) and his participation in the American Revolutionary War. It focused primarily on the life and adjacent families of the Reverend John W. Hamlin, the next-to youngest son of Ned and Dollie. It is currently out of print, but is a resource for those interested in specific details about that family line that settled in Brooklyn, New York and the turns experienced in their lives. It is reproduced here.

Reverend John W. Hamlin and wife, Frances Walker Hamlin

Daughters of Reverend John W. Hamlin and wife, Francis:
Irene, Gertrude and Hazel taken near their
Brooklyn, New York home.

# John W. Hamlin

## of Chesterfield County, Virginia

### His Ancestors and Descendants
### 1751-2008

by

Willie Jeanne Hamlin Kelly
&
Linda Hamlin Jones

# INTRODUCTION

**J**ohn William Hamlin was born into a world very different from the one from which he ultimately departed.

As an African American child of mixed heritage, he was the ninth child of Edward Yates Hamlin (a former slave holder), and Dolly Scott (his former slave). His birth in 1870 followed the tumultuous post civil war years, and his life was one of remarkable transition.

Over the next 67 years, John would journey from south to north, enslavement to freedom, country life to urban sophistication, and racial discrimination to spiritual leadership.

Although many of his grandchildren (now in the 70's and 80's) can recall visiting "grandpa," and attending Mount Lebanon Baptist Church in Brooklyn, New York where he pastored, most were too young to acquire more than one or two truly personal stories. And, typical of a time when "children were seen and not heard," few of this generation were enlightened about the heritage and ancestry of the Hamlin surname, or their lateral lines.

It was this desire to know more that prompted a focused examination of census reports, marriage certificates, land records, death certificates and ship manifests. Fortunately, the last five years of research has revealed much. This is an effort to share those findings.

This is also an invitation to our readers and relatives to share their knowledge of the Hamlin-Dinwiddie line; a heritage, like many similarly rooted American families, links with our country's history, as well.

# CHAPTER I

When John William Hamlin was born in 1870 in Dinwiddie County Virginia, the Civil War was only five years in the past, emancipation of the slaves had been proclaimed, and the records of his family heritage had already vanished.

The torching of the Richmond and Dinwiddie courthouses in that brutal North-South conflict destroyed all but a few pre-Revolutionary War documents. These included many irreplaceable papers that mapped the Virginia documentation of the Hamlin family from their February 25, 1638 land patent to the possible purchase of John's maternal enslaved ancestors. It would be another 140 years before any known segment of John's history would be committed to paper.

These losses, however, at that point in time, had already become irreversibly tragic events as the country struggled to reunite itself.

With his birth in 1870, John became the ninth child of **Edward "Ned" Yates Hamlin** (a former slaveholder) and **Dolly Scott** (his former slave) of Namozine Township in Dinwiddie County. Although unmarried, as prohibited under the stipulations of antebellum Virginia Law, Ned and Dolly were evidently both a committed couple and united family unit. They would ultimately have ten children by the time of Ned's passing in 1878. A previously unknown, first-born child named "Jim," born to Dolly on March 3, 1854 is included in this count.

Oral history states that Dolly actually saved Ned's life during the civil war when traversing soldiers invaded their farm. It is reported she successfully pleaded for his life stating that he was the father of their (at that time) six children. Ned's life was spared, and the couple would have four more children following the war. Their children included: Jim, Mary, Robert, Horace, Albert, Edgar, Patrick, Elvira, John and Walter.

Consistent with mandatory appearances, the 1870 Federal Census records (Plate 1) for Dinwiddie County presents an image of two separate Hamlin and Scott households. Up to this point, John and his siblings are listed under the surname, "Scott." However, a description of the "mulatto" children, the proximity of the homes, and John's first-hand knowledge of his father Ned, confirms theirs was, in fact, one single family unit.

By 1880 (Plate 2), however, John and his siblings carry the name, "Hamblin," a surname deeply rooted in the history of Virginia and the early settlement of the county. (See Chapter 2 for further information about the Hamblin, Hamlen, Hamblyn, Hamlin family.)

There is a tremendous lack of information, however, about the ancestors of Dolly Scott. What little is known is detailed below.

# THE SCOTT FAMILY

As with most families whose ancestors were once enslaved, diligence and commitment are needed to find confirmed evidence of family origins. This search is still ongoing for Dolly's ancestors.

What research *has* revealed is the apparent mother-daughter relationship of Sallie Scott (born in 1800) and Dolly (born 1833). Both women share a surname and a household in 1870 and 1880. Sallie is 33 years older than Dolly, an age consistent enough to qualify as Dolly's possible mother.

Remarkably, Sallie Scott enjoyed a long-life of 84 years, and it was a great discovery to find her exact date of death, January 20, 1884, in the Dinwiddie Register of Deaths (Plate 3), with Cause of Death listed as "Consumption." What further ties Sallie to Dolly, however, is the notation that Dolly's third oldest son, Robert E. Hamlin, was the "Person Giving Information of Death." Unexplainably, the form lists Robert's relationship with Sallie as "Friend." Could it be that Robert did not know that Sallie was his grandmother? Or, was he seeking to retain some family privacy?

A clue to Sallie and Dolly's ancestry may be found in the history of the Jarrell Scott family, Ned's next-door neighbor. The Scott family has lived in Dinwiddie since the early 1800s and records also show their ownership of slaves.

Is it a coincidence that Jarrell Scott, next-door neighbor of Ned Hamlin, shares a surname with Dolly and Sallie? Was Sallie perhaps an offspring of the Jarrell Scott family? Did the Scott family once own both Sallie and Dolly, and both chose to retain the Scott surname? Perhaps, there is no relationship between the two Scott families. Further research will hopefully reveal more.

# CHAPTER 2

## *The Edward Y. Hamlin Line*

Edward Yates Hamlin is the descendant of a prosperous and well-established Virginia family whose paper trails can be traced back to the pre-Revolutionary War era. Ned was a lawyer by trade, as were his ancestors who, from Virginia's earliest history, had served as Court Clerks, Sheriffs, and legal representatives.

He received a law degree from Virginia's Hampton-Sydney College, and his knowledge of the law apparently allowed him to draw up a will, dated February 1867, that provided for Dolly and their descendants. In it, Ned bequeathed "a certain piece of land lying on the south side of Petersburg or River Road," and gave her "one loom, and spinning wheel, all my kitchen furniture, pots, ovens, etc..." This gift was indeed observed by the Virginia courts upon Ned's demise in 1878.

A 30-year gap, spanning only one generation, presently prevents a confirmed link between Ned Hamlin's family and Virginia's earliest Hamlin residents of the 1630's. It is strongly believed that further research will one day determine the ancestral tie.

However, what *is* currently documented, and confirmed in 2004 by the Daughters of the American Revolution (DAR), is John W.'s descendancy from Revolutionary War Patriot, **Stephen H. Hamlin** (b.

1753) and his wife, **Mary Browne Hamlin**, his contemporary.

*Extant documentation shows the following to be true:*

Edward "Ned" Hamlin was the son of **William B. Hamlin** of Dinwiddie County and **Mary Yates** of Lunenburg, Virginia. They married on October 5, 1810 and had three children Ned, Susan and William B., Jr.

In fact, William B. actually married four times. First to **Christian "Kitty" Burwell** in 1794; **Martha Goode** in 1799 and had a daughter Mary Ann Hamlin; Ned's mother, Mary Yates in 1810; and **Anner Patrick Boisseau** in about 1825 in Amelia, and had a son, James B. Hamlin.

William B. Hamlin, born in c. 1774, was the son of Stephen H. Hamlin and Mary Brown Hamlin as proven by the letter of marriage consent signed by William's mother in 1794 (Plate 4) permitting William to wed Kitty Burwell. Stephen had passed away prior to 1794.

Patriot **Stephen Henry Hamlin** (b. 1753), of Prince George County, Virginia did not carry arms, but as a farmer did provide certain critical goods for American Revolutionary Soldiers during the war. These included: 1 horse (age 6 years), 3 "beeves" (750 lbs. of beef), 3 sheep, 135 bushels of corn, 600 pounds of fodder and an additional 590 bushels of corn, as detailed in the Virginia Revolutionary Publick Claims in three volumes, pp. 29, 50, 316 and 319.

# THE YATES FAMILY

Further research also reveals that Ned's mother, Mary D. Yates, was the daughter of **Edmund Yates** and **Elizabeth Murray Yates**. Her grandfather was the Reverend **William Yates**, the fifth President of **William and Mary College** who served during the years 1761-1764.

William Yeats was an Anglican clergyman, rector of Abingdon Parish, Gloucester, and Bruton Parish; as well as a member of the Governor's Council. Further research will undoubtedly trace the family roots back to London, England.

# CHAPTER 3

Census documentation shows that John W. was 9 years of age when his father Edward Y. passed away. Although Ned provided for Dolly and her children in an 1866 will that included 132 acres of land and certain household goods, John decided to strike out on his own in 1888, when he reached 18. With his departure, he would never reside in his native Dinwiddie again.

According to oral history, John headed first for Virginia's Isle of Wight. As an energetic youth, it is said that he enjoyed exhibiting his athletic skill and natural grace by tap dancing on the top of empty wooden barrels.

Seven years later, in 1895, John had matured into a husband and father, living further north in Berryville, Virginia with his wife, **Frances Walker**.

## *The Walker Family*

John's wife Frances was the sixth child of **Jackson Walker** and **Susan Gray** Walker (Plate 5) of Berryville, Virginia and Battletown Township, Clarke County in West Virginia. In 1880, their family included, Marshall (22), Mary (20), George (17), Betsey (15), Joseph (12), Fanney/Frances (12), Bertie (9) and Charles (4).

The surnames Walker and Gray are commonly known to have Native American ties, and further research is planned to determine possible Indian ancestry.

It is also believed that the Walker family was once enslaved by **Edward Smith** since no documentation prior to 1870 can be found. The 1870 Federal Census is the first to name every American resident, including former slaves. The names of slaves were not listed on any of the eight prior federal census reports, including those of 1790, 1800, 1810, 1820, 1830, 1840, 1850 and 1860.

The Smith family members were large and prosperous landowners, and their acreage ultimately straddled the Virginia and West Virginia borders with the division of the state in 1863.

It is not uncommon to find former slaves living directly next-door to their former slaveholders and the Walkers seem not to be an exception. The 1870 Federal census documents one of the Walker children, oldest child Marshall Walker (13 years old), in the Smith household and identified as a "household Servant". By 1880, Marshal is found living with his parents and siblings.


## LIFE IN BERRYVILLE, VIRGINIA

It is logical to assume that John and Frances Hamlin (Plate 6), most likely lived in the Walker's hometown of Berryville during their early married years since their two oldest children, Susan (b. 1895) and John Francis (b. 1899) were the only two born in Virginia.

Even after the couple moved to Shrewsbury Township in Red Bank, New Jersey and then to Brooklyn, New York, John's sister-in-law, **Bertie Walker Willis**, remained close to her sister Frances, and would travel north to pay frequent visits.

In a remarkable find, a vintage picture of "Bert" Willis (Plate #7 & #8) was recently discovered in a book, "Berryville Celebrates! 1798-1998" by the Clarke County Historical Association, p. 69. It details the history of Berryville, including the township of **Josephine City**, which was founded in 1870. Josephine City evolved into an independent hamlet whose stores, schools, churches, cemeteries, and illumination fixtures were solely owned and operated by People of Color. Bert was a member of the "Women's Union Light Company" whose job it was to attend to and light the lamps located both east and west of the railroad tracks which ran through town.

Today, a small road still leads through what was once the town's main street, directly past the **Zion Baptist Church**, and into the aged **Milton Valley Cemetery**. It is believed that Bert, her husband, Andrew Willis, and their children Jackson, Andrew & Catherine are all quite possibly buried there.

Contact has been made with the **Clarke County African-American Museum and Cultural Center**, also known as the **Josephine School Community Museum**. It is hoped this organization will help further on-going efforts to find the final resting places of Jackson Walker, Suzie Gray Walker and their children.

# CHAPTER 4

It was reportedly not long after John and Frances married that John's life reached a major turning point with his decision to commit himself to God and the church.

## *Relocation to Red Bank, New Jersey*

John pursued this commitment by studying for, and successfully receiving, his license to preach in 1898. The Rev. John Hamlin devoted the next 20 years of his life to the spiritual goals and institutional growth of both the **Second Baptist Church** in Wayne, Pennsylvania and the **Calvary Baptist Church** in Red Bank, New Jersey, where John was ordained.

His career flourished as the Reverend Hamlin became one of the founders of the *Sea Coast Missionary Baptist Association* and where his efforts helped to burn the mortgage on the affiliated **Middletown Baptist Church.**

The family of John and Frances grew as well, with the New Jersey births of seven more children. These included: Irene (b. 1902), Gertrude (b. 1903) and Ella Hazel (b. 1904) (Plate #9); William (b. 1909) (Plate #10), James (b. 1906-1926), Catherine (b. 1913-1914), and Semiramis (1901–1901).

In 1916, the large family relocated to Brooklyn, New York when Reverend John (Plate #11) decided to accept an offer to Pastor the Mount Lebanon Baptist Church. Brooklyn would become home for the family over the next 22 years.

# CHAPTER 5

John, Frances and their six children arrived in Brooklyn on October 16, 1916, and lived at 1546 Bergen Street before moving into the church parsonage at 91 Sackman Street, a building that still stands today.

It was from this location that their children matured, married, and settled into their own homes in Brooklyn's township of Bedford, which would eventually become known as Bedford Stuyvesant.

Eldest son John was the first to wed. In 1920 he married **Wilhelmina Johnson** (Plate 13) and by 1930 became father to six children (Plates 14 & Plates 15): John, Catherine, Dorothy, Irene, Thelma and Wilhelmina (aka *Shing*). (See Chapter 6 for Johnson family history.)

In the years that followed, son William married **Harriet "Hattie" Miller** and became father to six children: William, Joan, Carroll, Paul, Pauline and Gregory (Plate #16). Daughter Ella Hazel married **Dr. Paul L. Jones** in 1935, and daughter Irene became mother to Bonnie Nelson in 1943 (Plate #17).

Daughter Gertrude and **Russell Greene** married in the 1920s and became parents to Gertrude (aka *Princess*) (Plate #18) and James (aka *Jimmy*) (Plate #19). Their daughter Princess would eventually grow up and marry **Robert Washington** of Chicago, and become parents to three children: William Robert Washington, Jr., Nevin and Pandora

Washington. Son Jimmy, would marry **Ethel "Lee" Kovac** and have three children: Paul, Russell and Gertrude Greene.

An interesting history waits to be uncovered with regard to the above descendants of Greene family ancestry. Oral history has it that Russell's parents were part of the Shinnacock Indian Tribe, and that somewhere in their history the family surname was once **Bunn**. This is a well-known surname affiliated with these eastern Long Island Native Americans. The family ancestors are also believed to have resided on the tribal reservation. Oral history and further diligent study may one day clarify this belief.

Over the subsequent years, as John and Frances were blessed with 15 grandchildren, Reverend John continued to meet with great success in leading the then-small Mount Lebanon church congregation. He increased membership from 75 to more than 1,000, and was instrumental in the creation of the *Eastern Baptist Association*, which still thrives today. During this time period, he also authored a book of special sermons and questions, a copy of which has not yet been successfully located.

# Plate # 1

The children of Edward Hamlin and Dolly Scott carry their mother's surname in 1870.

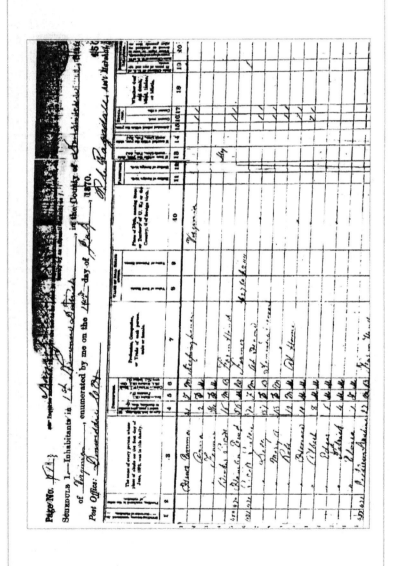

Plate # 2

**The 1880 census for Namozine Township, Dinwiddie County, lists the children of Edward & Dolly with their rightful surname, "Hamlin."**

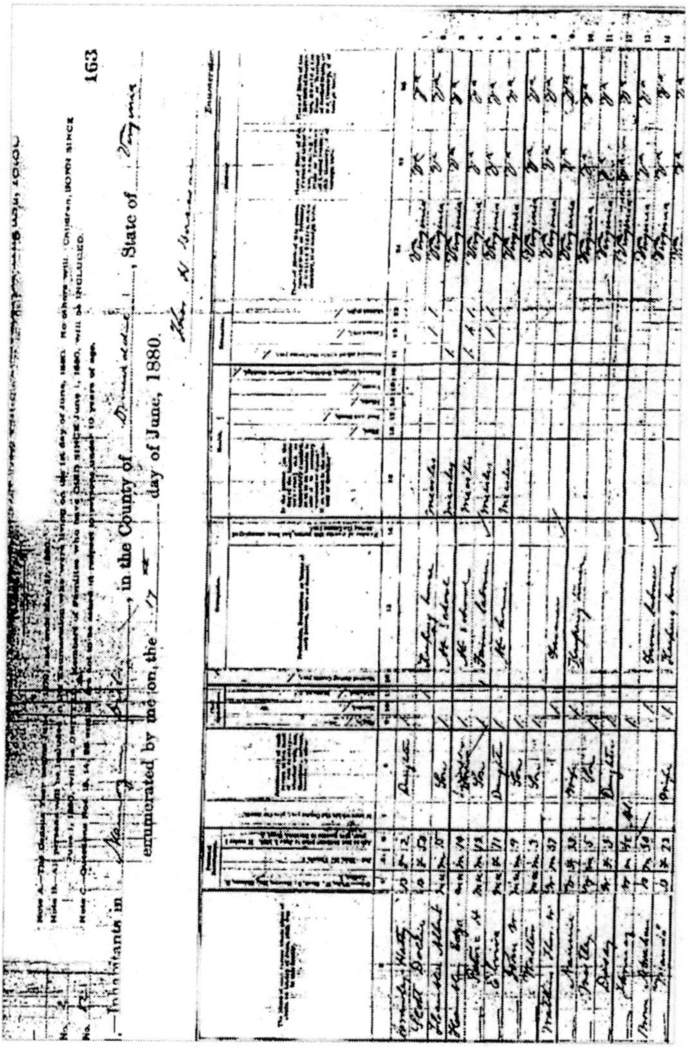

## Plate # 3

Dolly's mother, Sallie Scott (shown underlined), is found in the
1884 Register of Deaths for Dinwiddie, Virginia.

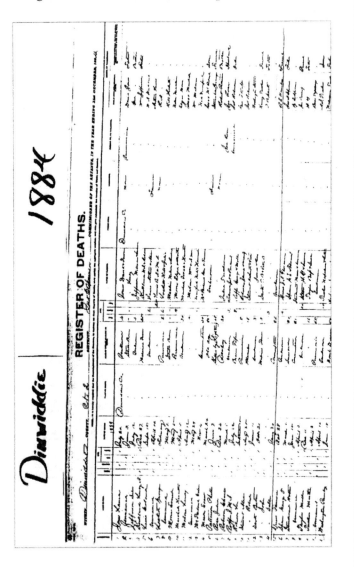

## Plate # 4

Mary Hamlin's 1794 Letter of Consent issues permission for her
son, William B. Hamlin, to marry Miss Kitty Burwell, his first wife.

## Plate # 5

**The 1880 family of Jackson Walker and Susan Gray Walker
lived in the Osborn District of Jefferson County, West Virginia.**

W426

Walker, Jackson
(HEAD OF FAMILY)

**WEST VIRGINIA**

VOL 5    E.D. 6

SHEET 43    LINE 40

| Mu | m | 52 |
|----|----|----|
| (COLOR) | (SEX) | (AGE) |

Va.

Jefferson
(COUNTY)

(BIRTHPLACE)
Osburn Dist
(M. C. D.)

(CITY)    (STREET)    (HOUSE NO.)

### OTHER MEMBERS OF FAMILY

| NAME | RELATION-SHIP | AGE | BIRTHPLACE |
|------|---------------|-----|------------|
| Walker, Susan | W | 44 | Va. |
| Walker, Marshal | S | 22 | Va. |
| Walker, Mary | D | 20 | Va. |
| Walker, George | S | 17 | Va. |
| Walker, Betsey | D | 15 | West Va. |

1880 CENSUS - INDEX
DEPARTMENT OF COMMERCE #1, See #2
BUREAU OF THE CENSUS

A-1a

Walker, Jackson
(HEAD OF FAMILY—CONTINUED)

STATE West Virginia

### OTHER MEMBERS OF FAMILY—CONTINUED

| NAME | RELATION-SHIP | AGE | BIRTHPLACE |
|------|---------------|-----|------------|
| Walker, Joseph | S | 12 | West Va. |
| Walker, Fanny | D | 12 | West Va. |
| Walker, Bestie | D | 9 | West Va. |
| Walker, Charles | S | 4 | West Va. |

Plate # 6
John W. Hamlin and wife, Frances Walker Hamlin.

Plate # 7
Bert Walker Willis (rear, far left) with Women's Union Light Company in Josephine City, Berryville, Virginia at the turn-of-the-century.

**Plate # 8**
Enlarged image of Bert Willis, sister of Frances Walker Hamlin.

**Plate # 9**
Gertrude, Ella Hazel and Irene Hamlin, daughters of
Rev. John W. and Frances Hamlin.

Plate # 10
William Hamlin, youngest son of John and Frances, in his
World War II US Army uniform.

Plate # 11
Rev. John Hamlin and wife Frances moved to
Brooklyn, New York in 1916.

**Plate # 12**
Eldest son, John Francis Hamlin (born 1899) as a young man.

**Plate # 13**
Wilhelmina Johnson Hamlin, wife of John F. Hamlin, c. 1925

Plate # 14
John W. Hamlin, with youngest sisters Thelma and Shing.

Plate # 15
Sisters (l to r) Catherine, Irene and Dorothy Hamlin.

**Plate # 16**
**Hattie Miller Hamlin with children (l to r)**
**Billy, Carroll and Joan Hamlin.**

**Plate # 17**
**Infant Bonnie Nelson in 1943.**

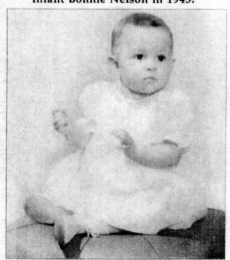

**Plate # 18**
**Russell Greene with daughter Gertrude,**
**nicknamed "Princess."**

**Plate # 19**
**Jimmy Greene, son of Russell Greene and Gertrude Hamlin Greene.**

**Plate # 20**
Siblings, John Henry and Wilhelmina Johnson, children of
William Henry Johnson and Catherine Cannon Qualter Johnson.

## Plate # 21
Record of marriage for William H. Johnson and Catherine Qualter on September 11, 1899 at Concord Baptist Church in Brooklyn.

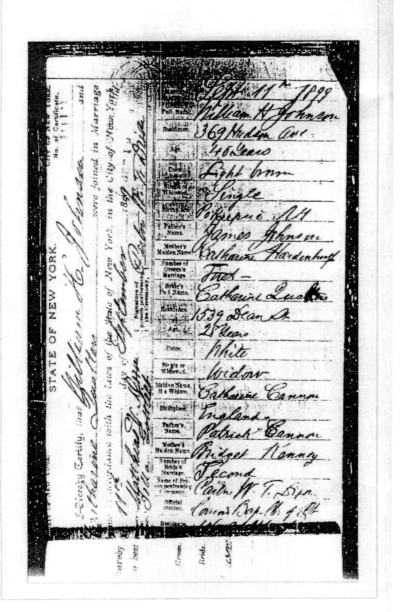

**Plate # 22**
Howard Colored Orphanage in Brooklyn, New York prior to the
institution's move to Kings Park, Suffolk County, Long Island.

# Plate # 23

Map of Historic Weeksville in Brooklyn, NY. (Source: "Weeksville Then and Now" by Joan Maynard and Gwen Cottman, p. 45).

Hunterfly Road was once an old Indian trail that dates back more than 300 years, and traversed from south to north from Jamaica Bay to what would become, Brooklyn's Navy Yard.

## HISTORIC WEEKSVILLE

1. Hunterfly Road Houses
2. Site of James Weeks House
3a. Bethel Tabernacle A.M.E. Church
 b. Present location
4. Site of African Civilization Society
5a. Site of Zion Home for the Colored Aged
 b. Site of Home in 1892
 c. Brooklyn Home for the Aged
6a. Howard Orphanage, early site,
 b. Expanded site

7a. Site of Colored School #2-1847
 b. Site of Colored School #2-1886
 c. Weeksville School, present site
8. Site original P.S. #83
 Later site P.S. #83 (Same as 3b)
9a. Site Berean Church, 1851
 b. Present site Berean Church
10. Site 1968/69 Archeological Dig
 Present Weeksville Gardens Houses
11. Original site of St. Phillips Church
12. Our Lady of Charity Church

Map: Pratt Center for Community & Environmental Development and Joan Maynard.

**Plate # 24**
Catherine Cannon was buried with her son, John Henry Johnson,
upon her death in 1930. Her epitaph is inscribed on the reverse
side of her son's stone.

**Plate # 25**
Children of John F. Hamlin and Wilhelmina Johnson Hamlin, as adults: (l to r) Catherine, Dorothy, Irene, Thelma, Shing and John.

Plate # 26
Headstone at New Jersey's White Ridge Cemetery
in Eatontown marks the graves of John W. Hamlin, his wife
Frances and four of their children.

# CHAPTER 6

John Francis Hamlin and Wilhelmina Johnson were youngsters of 21 and 17 when they wed in 1920. By 1930 they would become the parents of six children. Tragically, Wilhelmina passed away that same year on April 10, 1930 just months before her 27th birthday.

John would eventually remarry, taking the former **Helen Crooke** as his second wife in 1933. They would remain wedded for 33 years until John's passing in 1966. Helen died in November of 1981.

A quiet and soft-spoken man, "DAD-duh," as his five daughters called him, seldom spoke of their mother Wilhelmina (also nicknamed, *Bill*) in the years following her death. Precious little was known of their mother's parentage or history, and it was only through recent research that this history was discovered.

In fact, even the graves of Wilhelmina's mother, father and brother were only recently located. Following is a portion of those ancestral findings.

## *The Johnson Family of Poughkeepsie*

Wilhelmina was born in Brooklyn, New York and was the first of two children born to **William H. Johnson** (b. 1860) and his wife, **Catherine Cannon Qualter Johnson** (b. 1866). Wilhelmina was born in July 30, 1903, and her brother, John Henry Johnson, arrived on September 4, 1904 (Plate 20).

Their father William is found with his parents as a three-month-old infant on the 1860 Federal Census for Poughkeepsie, New York. In that year, William's father, **James Johnson**, a native New Yorker of (age 26), worked as a "Boatman." His mother, Catharine Hardenburg Johnson, also a born New Yorker, was 24 and kept house.

The 1850 federal census for Fishkill Township in Dutchess County, New York, reveals that James Johnson was the second of five children of **Jacob Johnson** (b. 1810) and his wife **Ellen Johnson** (b. 1812). Their children included: Henry (b. 1832), James (b. 1833), Jacob, Jr. (b. 1836), ~~Mary~~ (b. 1838) *Margaret* and Betsy (b. 1842).

Research on the Johnson family is hampered by the fact of their birth during the transitional years following New York's 1827 elimination of statewide slavery. Although welcomed, this edict had not yet afforded equal freedoms to all People of Color, and quite possibly explains an inability to locate the family on the 1840 and 1830 census reports. Perhaps, at that time, People of Color were simply left uncounted, a practice carried over from the slave years.

One remarkable find is the 1850 listing of a **George Hardenbergh** (b. 1798) with wife **Elizabeth Hardenbergh** (b. 1797) and son Charles (17 years) living in the same Fishkill Township as Jacob Johnson and his family. Perhaps, William's parents – James Johnson and Catherine Hardenbergh – met while living in Fishkill.

Another research consideration is the location of

an M. Hardenbergh (15/f/b) and an E. Johnson (25/f/b) living only four doors away from the George Hardenbergh family listed above. They are both working for **John Diddell** (77/m/w), a wealthy farmer and former slaveholder. Could it be that both the Johnson and Hardenberg families were once the property of John Diddell? Are M. Hardenbergh and E. Johnson perhaps related to William's parents? The search for answers continues.

What is known is that the Dutch were among the earliest settlers both in the state's Hudson Valley, and New York City (formerly known as New Amsterdam). It is hoped that examination of early land-ownership records, one of the largest being the huge "Great Hardenbergh Land Patent," will help narrow that search.

Catharine's maiden name suggests she may have been of mixed ancestry, and perhaps further research of the Hardenburg name may one day confirm her parentage.

By 1870, however, James cannot be found in any documentation. It is quite possible he was killed in the Civil War. Perhaps he was a member of the United States Colored Troops (USCT), a segregated military unit formed in May of 1863 by government order. Microfilmed records of archival military service papers are gradually becoming available, and it will inevitably become a slow process to examine all servicemen of color named, *James Johnson*. In spite of this challenge, however, plans are currently in place to attempt to locate him.

## *Working for the Secretary of State*
## *of New York*

Catharine Hardenburg Johnson, and her son William, however, *are* documented in the 1870 census. Remarkably, they are found living in the household of **Homer A. Nelson**, Secretary of State of New York. Catharine is working as a "Domestic," and her son William (at 11 years old) is a "Servant."

How did Catharine come into such a position of trust? What references did she possess to gain the employ of this noted New Yorker?

By 1880, however, only ten years later when the next federal census is compiled, both Catharine and William are missing. The census taker will sometimes miss entire blocks or farms due to inclement weather, or an unwillingness to perform the full duties of the job. Perhaps, this explains their absence from the record books.

A massive fire destroyed the storage facility of the 1890 federal census, and there remains a huge gap of time for all researchers where valuable information remains lost.

It is with the *next* available census that forty-year-old William re-emerges in 1900 wedded to Catherine Cannon Qualter (28), a widowed mother of two daughters, who emigrated from England to the United States soon after the Civil War.

# The Cannon Kenny Family of England and Ireland

*John*

Catherine Cannon was the sixth child of **Patrick Cannon** (b. 1830) and **Bridget Kenny** (b. 1833). She arrived in New York with her mother and siblings Anna (11), Mary (9), Margaret (8), Michael (5) and James (2) on the *SS Chicago*, which departed from the Liverpool dock and arrived on September 30, 1867. Kate was the youngest at only a year old.

Their father Patrick preceded them on the **SS Palmyra** and arrived in New York on March 26, 1867 to prepare for his family's arrival.

Although Kate and her siblings were born in England, both her parents were born in Ireland. The Irish Potato Famine, which spanned the years of 1846-1850, may have forced them to leave. Undoubtedly, a remarkable project of discovery awaits the family member willing to explore the circumstances of Patrick and Bridget's departure from their native home.

Upon their arrival in America, the Cannon family settled in Long Island City, known in 1870 as Newtown, Long Island. From there, they resided for a time in the township's Third Street. Eventually, they moved to the Brooklyn neighborhood of Greenpoint. Over time, Kate's brother Michael worked in a Tin Shop, and then as a New York City fireman. Sister Mary was employed as a Seamstress.

Records show that Kate married **Robert Qualter** in the 1880s. Robert was also born in England, and it is believed that the Qualter and Cannon families may have been friends from the "old country."

Together, Kate and Robert had 12 children, which included a set of triplets, two of whom did not survive infancy. In fact, only three of Kate's children survived childhood: Mary, Anna and Rose Qualter. Of these surviving three, Mary unfortunately died at the age of 13, while still attending school.

The girls boarded at the Roman Catholic School, **St. Francis of Assisium Convent of Mercy** located on Willoughby Street and Classon Avenue. Perhaps a boarding school education was part of Kate's own educational experience. Unfortunately, their father Robert did not live to see them reach adulthood when he suffered an untimely death at age 30 on Christmas Day in 1896. It is a sad thought to consider that the children were most likely home from school for the holidays when this occurred.

Following a widowhood of three years, Kate met William H. Johnson. On September 11, 1899 Pastor William T. Dixon of **Concord Baptist Church** married the couple (Plate 21). In 1905 the couple lived in a wood frame home at 455 Hudson Street in downtown Brooklyn with their children Wilhelmina and John ~~were living in 1905~~.

Old Brooklyn residence directories from the turn of the century show Kate and William eventually moved to other Brooklyn addresses in subsequent years, including 253 Chauncey Street and 300 Chauncey Street. Before her marriage to William, Kate lived at 1539 Dean Street. This residence was located across the street from the historic **Brooklyn Howard Colored Orphanage** at Dean Street and Troy Avenue.

This unique institution was founded in 1866 by Sarah Tillman, a woman of color who saw the need to house and care for the many children of color who had been orphaned during the Civil War. At the time, orphanages (even in New York) were strictly segregated, and black children were regularly refused admittance.

As an additional service, the Howard institution also agreed to room and board children who were not orphans in the strict sense, but who perhaps had only one surviving parent. This accommodation allowed widowed mothers to gain employment, often as a sleep-in servant, in the knowledge their children would be well cared for.

Although Wilhelmina and John were not orphaned, and actually had both their parents, both the 1910 and 1915 federal and state census documents list the children as "Inmates" of the Howard Colored Orphanage.

### The Move to Kings Park

A rendering of the Howard Orphanage (Plate 22) illustrates the front of the Brooklyn facility prior to the sale of both the building, lot and surrounding land. This institution was located in the Weeksville section of Brooklyn (Plate 23), an historic location marking the residence of most of Brooklyn's people of color, as well as African-American churches and schools dating back to the 1840's and 1850's. In 1911 the Howard Orphanage relocated to Kings Park, New York in Suffolk County, Long Island. Renamed the **Howard Orphanage and Industrial School**, its scope was broadened to include training in carpentry, animal husbandry and farming skills. This curriculum was fashioned after Booker T. Washington's Tuskegee Institute in Alabama, and in fact the orphanage enjoyed the charity and concern of Booker T., himself.

Unfortunately, adequate funding was always a constant issue with the running of the orphanage. An on-going series of dinners, fundraisers, and musical concerts were part of a ceaseless campaign to raise needed money. Ultimately, it was a series of tragic circumstances that conspired to force its final closing in 1918.

Thankfully, by that point in time, Wilhelmina and John had already left Kings Park and returned to Brooklyn where they attended P.S. 28, a public school still in operation on Herkimer Street.

It was around this time that Kate's other two children started lives of their own. On January 3, 1915 Kate's daughter, Anna Qualter, married **Elijah Willis**, a paint dealer, at **Our Lady of Mercy** in Brooklyn. Two years later, on November 28, 1917, Rose Qualter married **Arthur Disbrow**. Within a few years, in 1920, we find Anna and Elijah Willis living at 58 Utica Avenue with their two children, Robert

H. Willis (3 1/2 years) and Catherine Willis (one month). Rose and Arthur Disbrow lived at 418 Classon Avenue. Eventually, both couples moved to Long Island's Farmingville Township where they died and are buried.

## A Series of Deaths

On June 30, 1920,, Kate's husband William passed away, only a short time after Wilhelmina and John returned to the city from the orphanage. William is buried at the Linden Hill Cemetery in Maspeth, Queens.

Son, John, enrolled in the U.S. Navy on January 7, 1924, and died on April 17 of the same year in a tragic accident at Brooklyn's elevated Kosciusko Train Station. This occurred within only five days of his receiving an honorable discharge from the service (Plate 24).

Perhaps as a result of prolonged stress over the loss of her son, Kate herself died on January 18, 1930. It is a small mercy to know that Kate did not live to see her daughter, Wilhelmina, follow her three months later on April 10 of the same year.

Following research efforts by the family, Kate's unmarked grave was only recently discovered at the **National Military Cemetery** on Jamaica Avenue near the Brooklyn/Queens boarder, where she is buried with her son John (Plate 25). When informed of their omission, a new stone was speedily placed on the dual grave by the government to mark Kate's presence there. Daughter, Wilhelmina is at the Hamlin family plot at White Ridge Cemetery in Eatontown, New Jersey.

# CHAPTER 7

The dual loss of his wife, Wilhelmina, and then his mother-in-law, Kate, within months of each other must have placed enormous emotional strain upon young John.

Shortly thereafter, however, John's mother, Frances, had a stroke and also passed away on August 6, 1930 at age 58. With this tragedy, both John Francis and his father, John William, became widowers within months of each other.

It was a struggle for young John to hold his young family together in the face of a national depression. His sister Gertrude, and husband Russell, helped make this happen by caring for the five young daughters, all under the age of 10.

It is said that a suggestion was made to send the children to an orphanage, or to separate homes, in view of the loss of their mother. But, John would not hear of it. He adamantly insisted that the family be raised together. And, ultimately, they were.

It would be three years before John F. remarried. It was a strange twist of fate, that father and son both took second wives within one day of one another. Young John F. wed **Helen Crooke** on July 27, the day after his father, Rev. John, married **Cora Vaughan** on July 26, 1933.

It has recently come to light that Helen's father, **Peter Crooke** (b. 1869), was himself raised in the

Brooklyn Howard Colored Orphanage. He and his brother **Fred Crooke** are both listed as "Inmates" in the 1880 Federal Census for the institution. Like Wilhelmina, second wife Helen was also of mixed heritage, and her mother, **Margaret Johnson**, of Irish ancestry.

Eventually, in a large but successful struggle, John brought all six children to adulthood (Plate 26). And, with the start of World War II, they began to marry. Son John, a member of the US Marines and later a decorated New York City Fireman, married **Frances Johnson** and had four children: John, Pamela, Patricia and Leonard Hamlin.

John's daughters married as well. Catherine married **Mitchell Bryant**, also a Marine and friend of her brother John, and had Michael and Karen Bryant. Dorothy wed Tuskegee Airman and Mechanical Engineer, **George Rhodes**, and produced daughters Linda and Wilhelmena Rhodes. Irene married **Frank Jackson** and became mother to Rose, Lance and Cheryl Jackson. Thelma and **Vernon Lawless** became parents to daughter LaVerne Lawless. Thelma also wed **Austin Francis** (a decorated NY City Policeman). Youngest daughter, Shing and husband **James Washington**, became parents to Denise and Johnny Washington. In a second marriage, Shing later wed **Clifford Abraham** (Detective in the NY Police Department), and together have a daughter and son, Adrienne and Geoffrey Abraham.

In all, John F. Hamlin would count 16 grandchildren in his line of descendancy before he passed away on January 26, 1966. He is buried at Evergreen Cemetery located on the Brooklyn/Queens border.

The Reverend John Hamlin predeceased his son by 28 years, and was laid to rest on August 12, 1937 at the White Ridge Cemetery in Eatontown, New Jersey (Plate 27).

John's sisters and brother, for the most part, lived long fulfilling lives. Gertrude died in 1976, and husband Russell died in 1995. Brother William moved to Albany in the 1950s and died in 1975. His wife Hattie predeceased him on July 18, 1969. Sister Irene, who lived to see nearly 100 years of age, passed away on December 11, 1998. Ella Hazel and husband Dr. Paul L. Jones died within seven months of each other in 1983.

# Future Research

This short text details only the briefest overview of the grandchildren and "great-grands" of John W. Hamlin. It is not an attempt to even come close to retelling the lives of John W., his sisters and brothers, or his faintly known ancestors, now hundreds of years in the past. This is simply one segment of the Hamlin story; and its authors welcome the input and further research efforts of interested friends and relatives.

Readers are invited to contribute oral history, photos, and pertinent documentation to further expand the recorded history of the Dinwiddie line of the Hamlin American story. Our mailing address is: Post Office Box #3220032, Rosedale, NY 11422. And, e-mail contacts are: mena23219@msn.com and lmrhojo@~~aol.com~~ optimum.net We look forward to hearing from you.

Produced in Cooperation
with the
Weeksville Society
of
Brooklyn, New York.

CPSIA information can be obtained at www.ICGtesting.com
Printed in the USA
BVOW07s1202271014

372510BV00001B/3/P